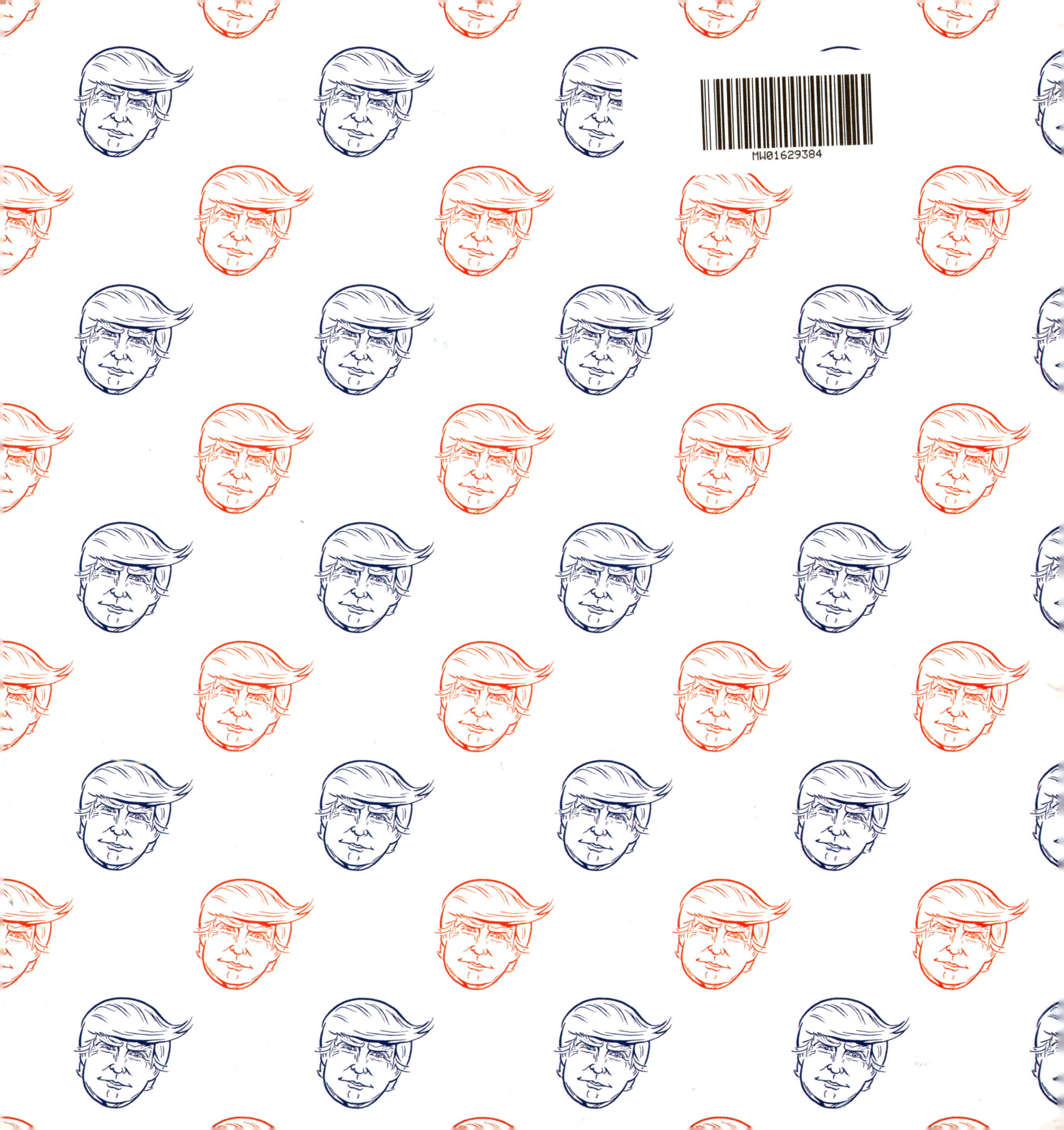

MW01629384

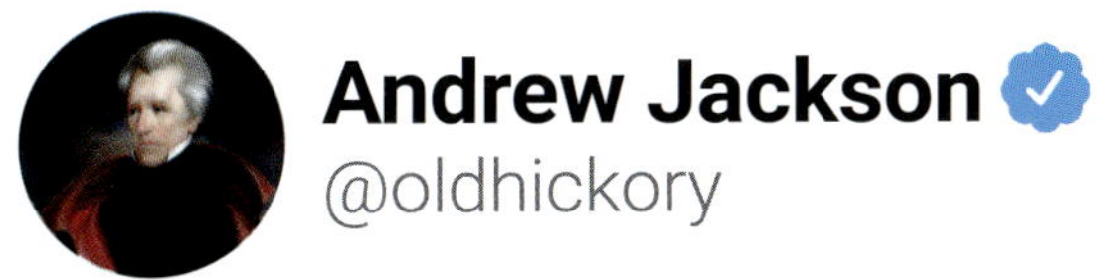

Andrew Jackson
@oldhickory
I was born for the storm, and a calm does not suit me.
3:17 PM · June 14, 1831

THE ART OF THE TWEET

theartofthetweet.com

This book is a collection of real Twitter tweets by Donald J. Trump, 45th President of the United States of America.
All tweets are real tweets from Donald J. Trump's verified Twitter account twitter.com/realDonaldTrump.
Web links, images, and other media have been omitted. Lengthy tweets over Twitter's character limit have
been condensed from multiple tweets into one tweet. Any spelling errors/typos are from the original tweet.
The intent of this book is to provide a consolidated historical record of Donald J. Trump's most influential, controversial,
and humorous tweets. We hope this book will spark a conversation around one of social media's most controversial public figures.
The Art of the Tweet is not authorized, affiliated, or in any way officially connected with Donald J. Trump,
Twitter, Inc., or any political party or political organization.

COVER ARTWORK BY BEN GARRISON

grrrgraphics.com

Printed in the United States of America

ISBN 978-0-578-88198-0

THE ART OF THE TWEET

Real tweets from @realDonaldTrump

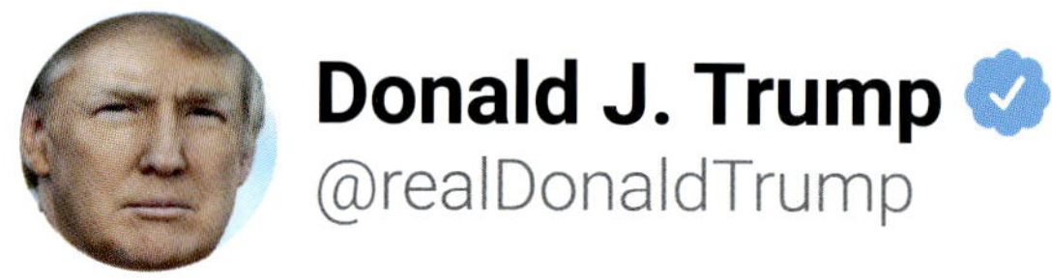

Donald J. Trump
@realDonaldTrump
"Know when to walk away from the table." The Art of the Deal
2:25 PM · Jul 27, 2011

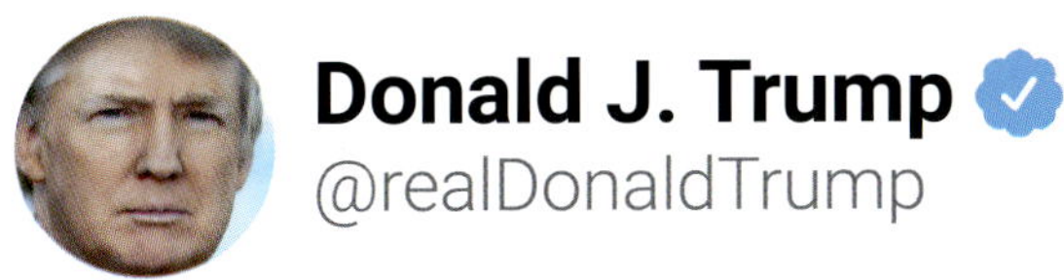

Donald J. Trump ✓
@realDonaldTrump

Barney Frank looked disgusting--nipples protruding--in his blue shirt before Congress. Very very disrespectful.

3:36 PM · Dec 21, 2011

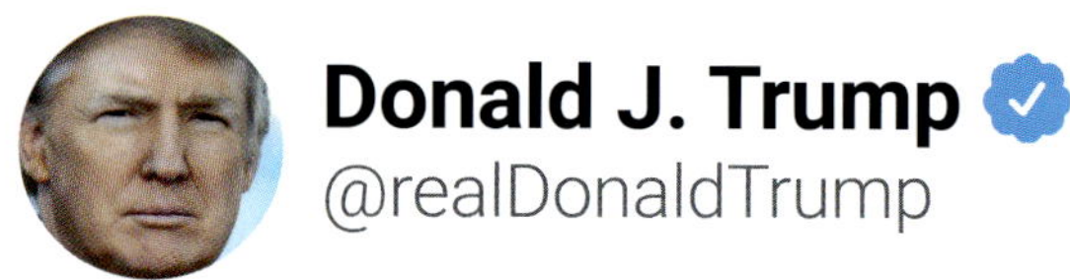

Donald J. Trump
@realDonaldTrump
"The Supreme Art of war is to subdue the enemy without fighting." -- Sun Tzu
11:04 AM • Jul 17, 2012

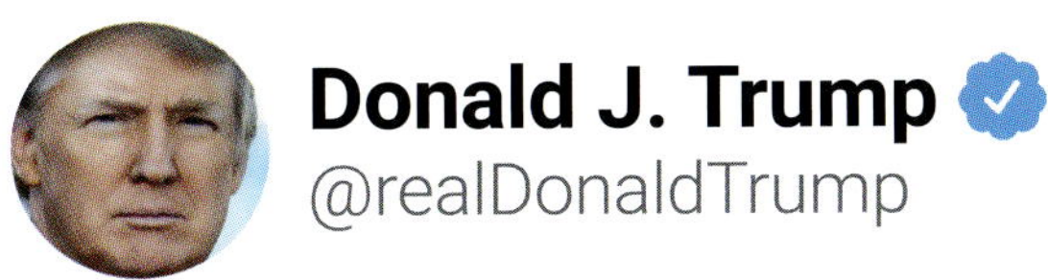

@ariannahuff is unattractive both inside and out. I fully understand why her former husband left her for a man- he made a good decision.

10:54 AM • Aug 28, 2012

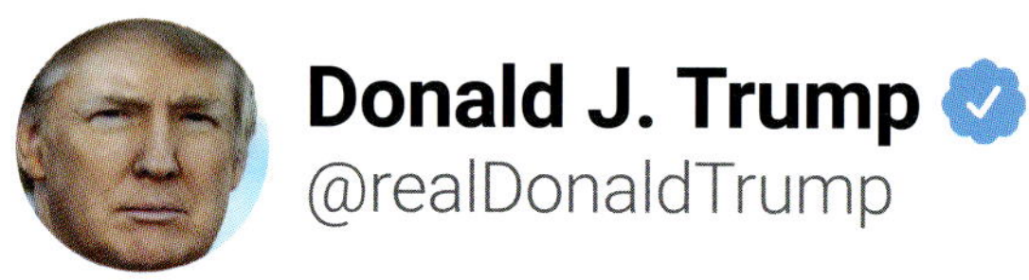

Donald J. Trump
@realDonaldTrump
Got to do something about these missing chidlren grabbed by the perverts. Too many incidents--fast trial, death penalty.
9:13 AM · Oct 8, 2012

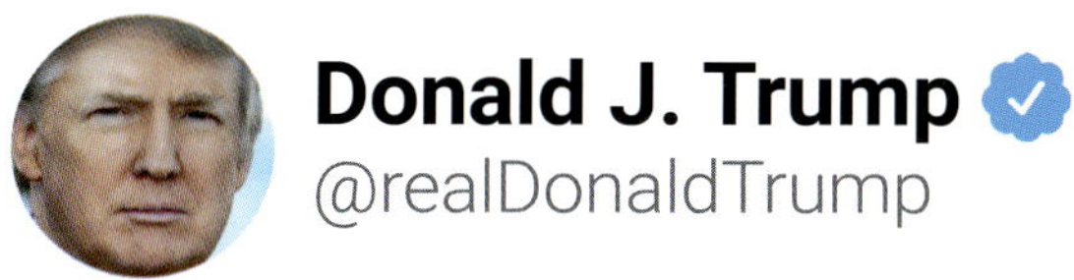

Donald J. Trump
@realDonaldTrump
I have never seen a thin person drinking Diet Coke.
2:43 PM • Oct 14, 2012

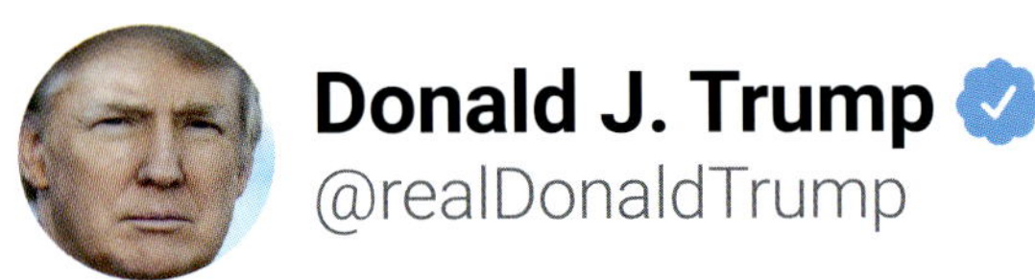

The Coca Cola company is not happy with me--that's okay, I'll still keep drinking that garbage.

1:47 PM • Oct 16, 2012

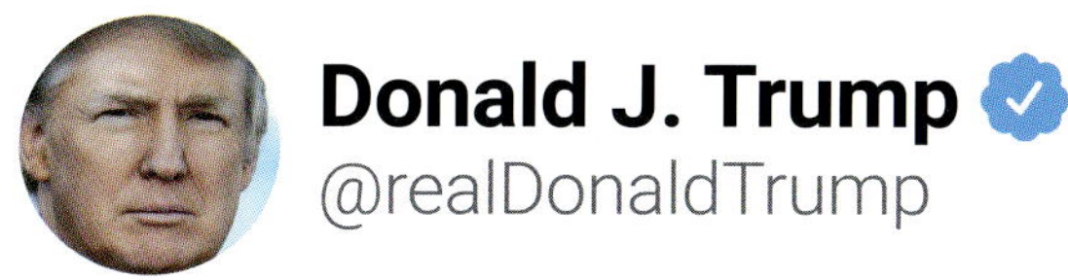

My twitter has become so powerful that I can actually make my enemies tell the truth.

11:06 AM • Oct 17, 2012

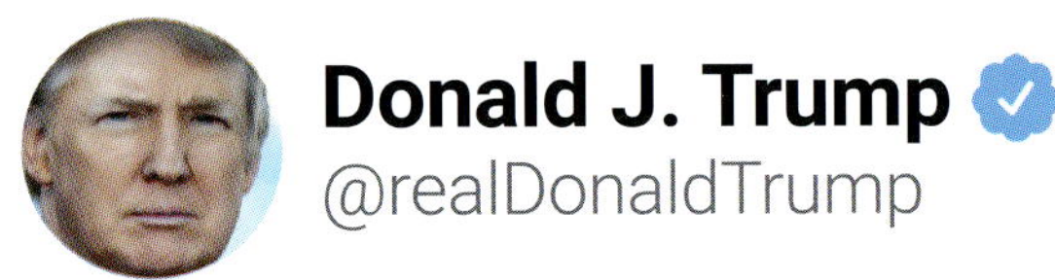

I never fall for scams. I am the only person who immediately walked out of my 'Ali G' interview

1:44 PM · Oct 30, 2012

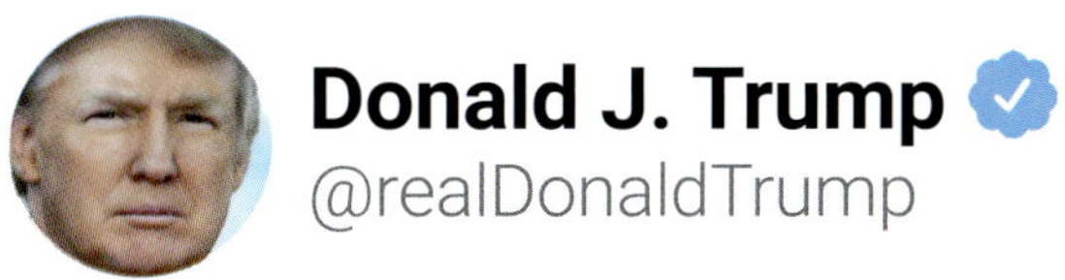

The concept of global warming was created by and for the Chinese in order to make U.S. manufacturing non-competitive.

2:15 PM · Nov 6, 2012

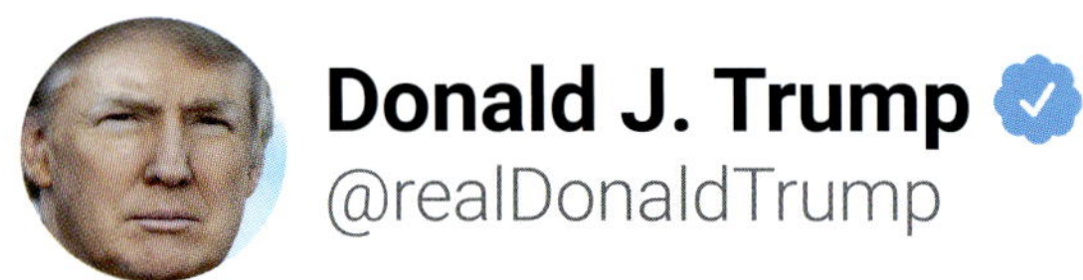

Pervert alert. @RepWeiner is back on twitter. All girls under the age of 18, block him immediately.

3:32 PM · Nov 7, 2012

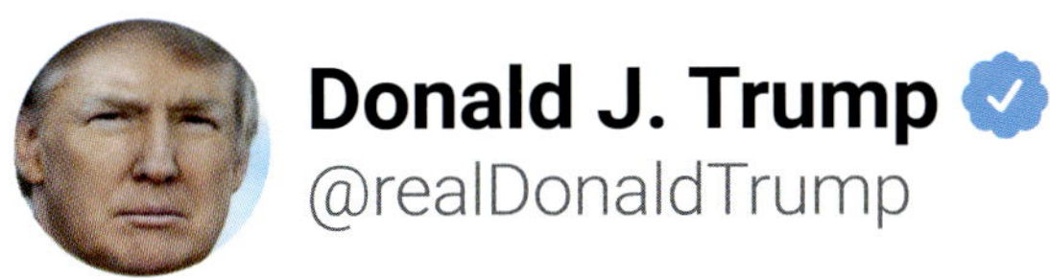

Donald J. Trump
@realDonaldTrump
I love Twitter.... it's like owning your own newspaper--- without the losses.
10:23 AM · Nov 10, 2012

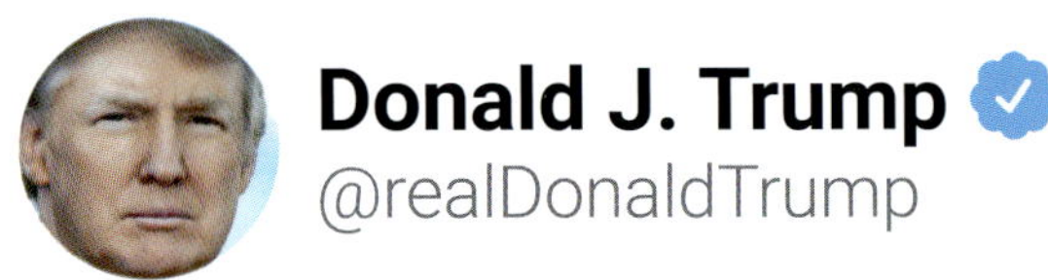

Donald J. Trump ✓
@realDonaldTrump

Thanks- many are saying I'm the best 140 character writer in the world. It's easy when it's fun.

10:23 AM · Nov 10, 2012

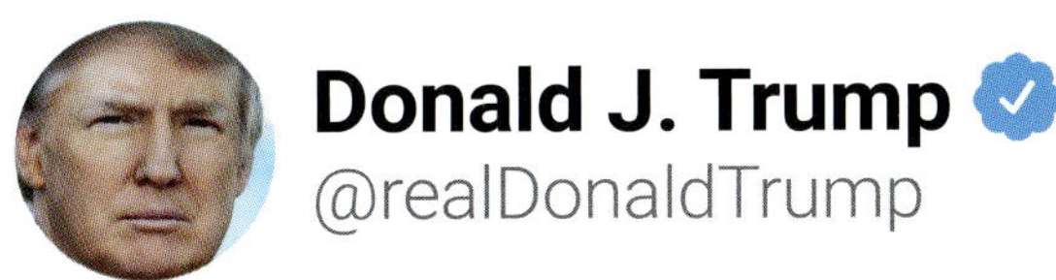

Donald J. Trump
@realDonaldTrump
It makes me feel so good to hit "sleazebags" back -- much better than seeing a psychiatrist (which I never have!)
11:06 AM · Nov 19, 2012

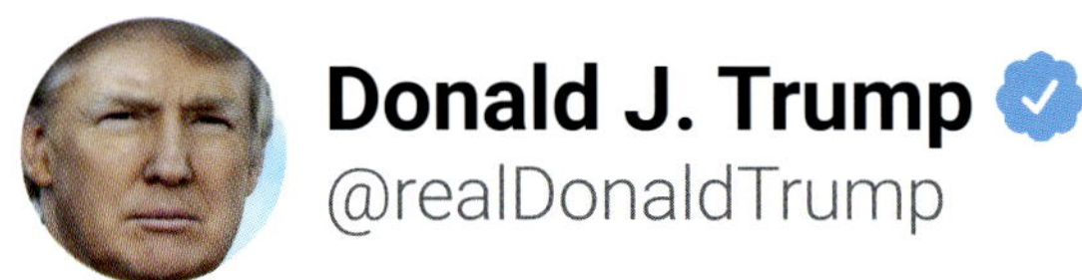

"You can't con people, at least not for long. If you don't deliver the goods, people will eventually catch on." - The Art of The Deal

4:50 PM • Dec 10, 2012

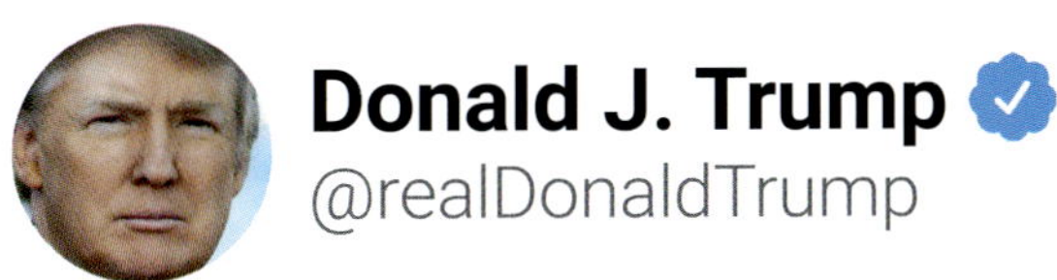

It's amazing that people can say such bad things about me but if I say bad things about them, it becomes a national incident.

3:24 PM · Jan 9, 2013

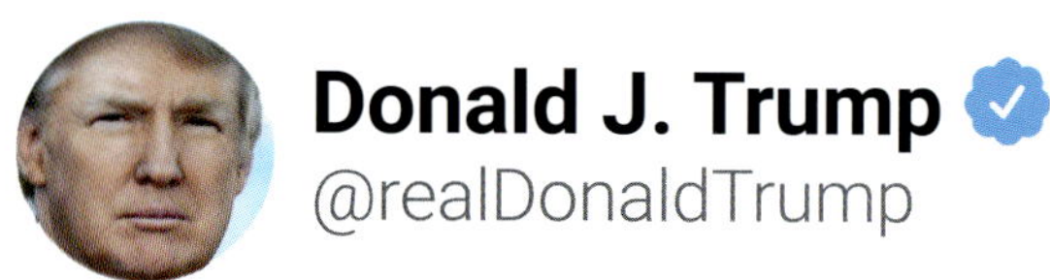

Donald J. Trump
@realDonaldTrump

I went to Wharton, made over $8 billion, employ thousands of people & get insulted by morons who can't get enough of me on twitter...!

4:34 PM • Feb 12, 2013

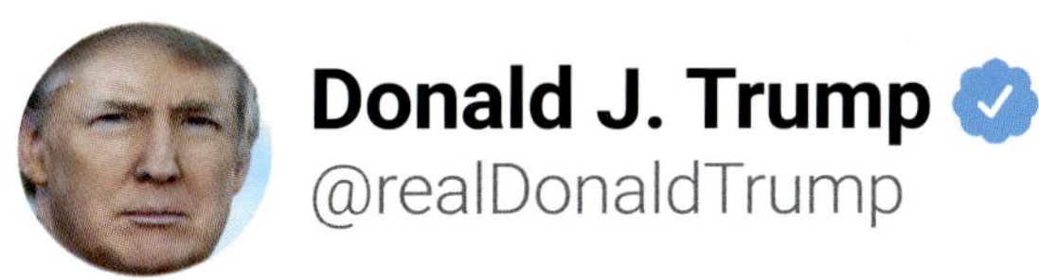

Donald J. Trump ✓
@realDonaldTrump

"Do not pray for easy lives. Pray to be stronger men." – Pres.
John F. Kennedy

4:48 PM · Feb 13, 2013

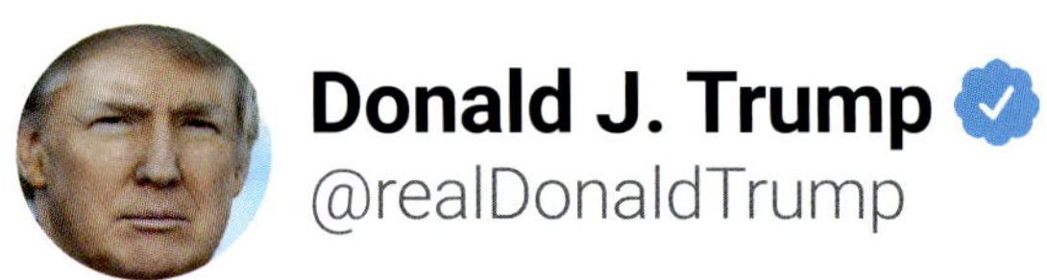

Donald J. Trump
@realDonaldTrump
"If the freedom of speech is taken away then dumb and silent we may be led, like sheep to the slaughter."
- George Washington
4:31 PM · Feb 15, 2013

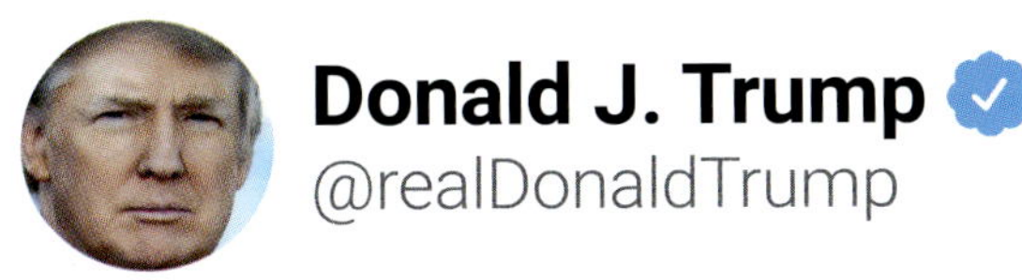

Donald J. Trump
@realDonaldTrump
China is not our friend. They are not our ally. They want to overtake us, and if we don't get smart and tough soon, they will.
3:35 PM · Feb 21, 2013

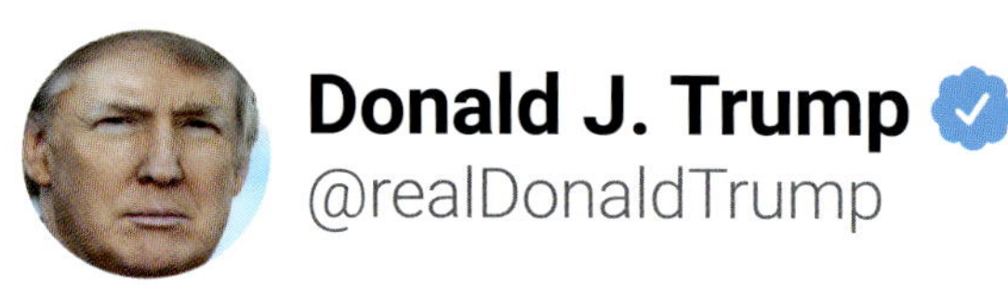

Donald J. Trump ✓
@realDonaldTrump

I know some of you may think I'm tough and harsh but actually I'm a very compassionate person (with a very high IQ) with strong common sense

10:05 AM · Apr 21, 2013

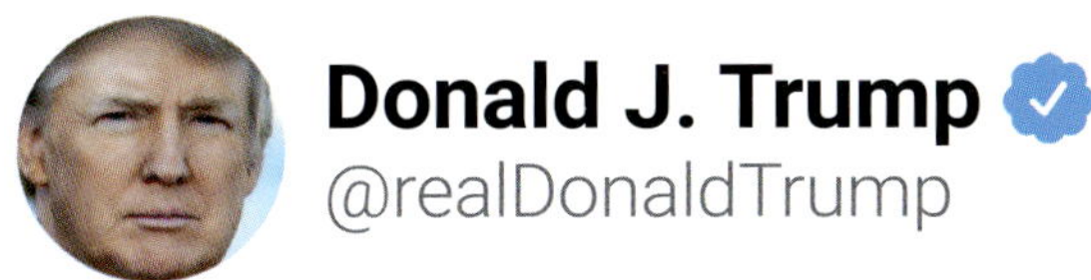

Donald J. Trump ✔
@realDonaldTrump

NO MERCY TO TERRORISTS you dumb bastards!

11:47 AM · Apr 21, 2013

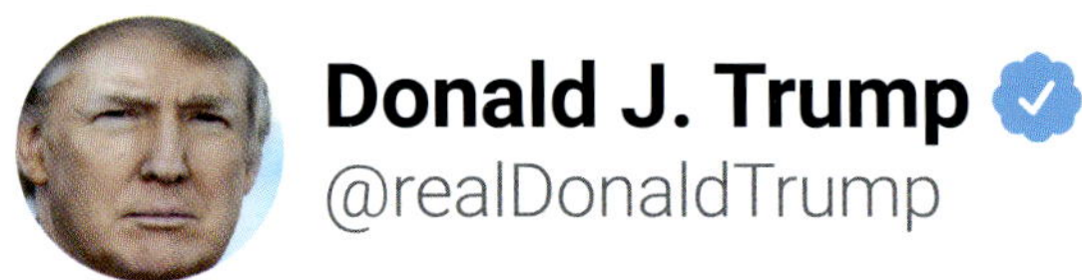

Donald J. Trump
@realDonaldTrump
Sorry losers and haters, but my I.Q. is one of the highest -and you all know it! Please don't feel so stupid or insecure,it's not your fault
9:37 PM · May 8, 2013

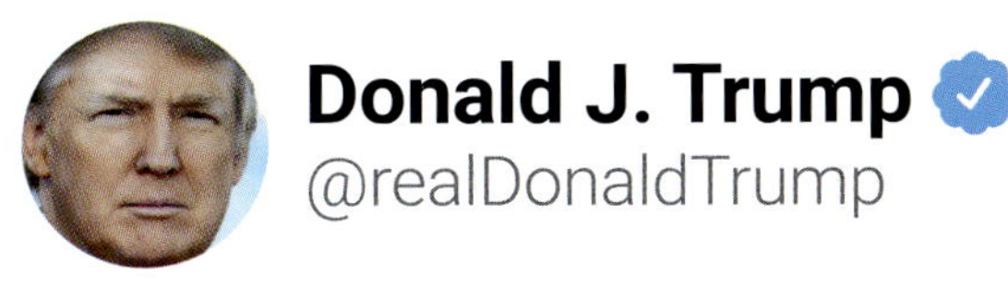

It's freezing outside, where the hell is "global warming"??

7:00 PM • May 25, 2013

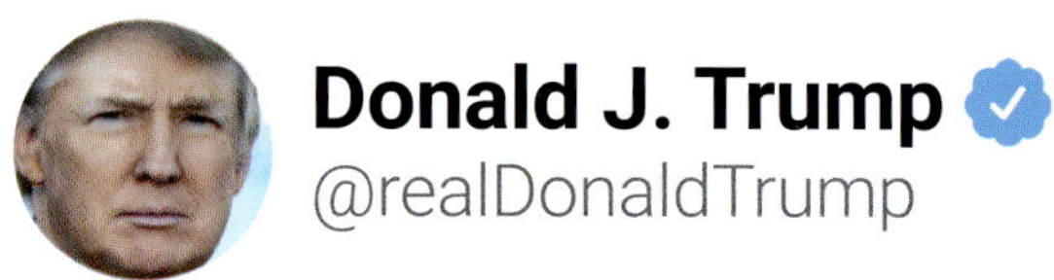

Donald J. Trump
@realDonaldTrump
Move slowly, carefully --- and then strike like the fastest animal on the planet!
1:11 AM · Sep 20, 2013

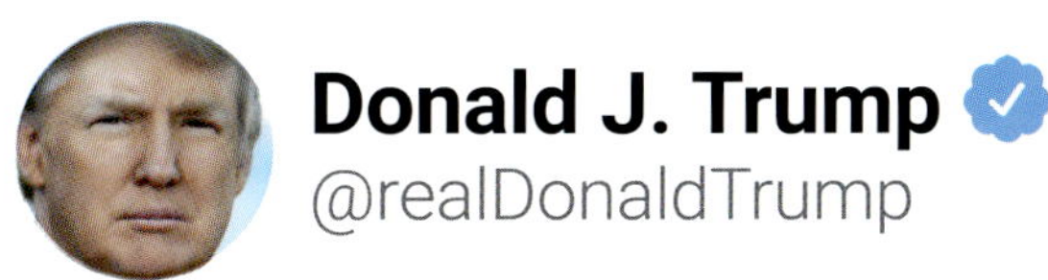

Donald J. Trump ✓
@realDonaldTrump

If you are lucky enough to catch a knockout assaulter before getting slugged, and you carry a gun, shoot the bastard (teach them a lesson)!

8:15 PM · Nov 21, 2013

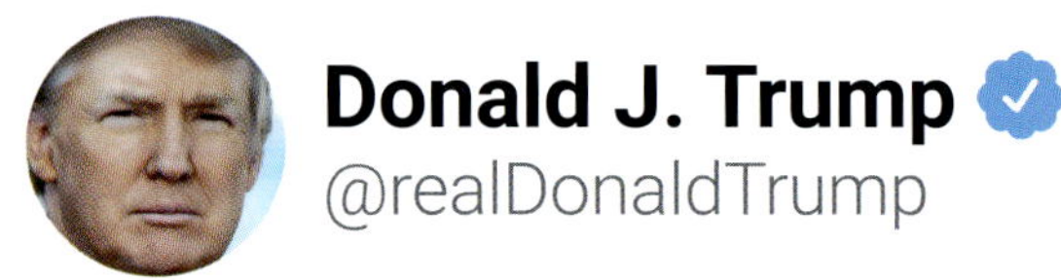

I hope we never find life on another planet because if we do there's no doubt that the United States will start sending them money!

6:34 AM • Jan 16, 2014

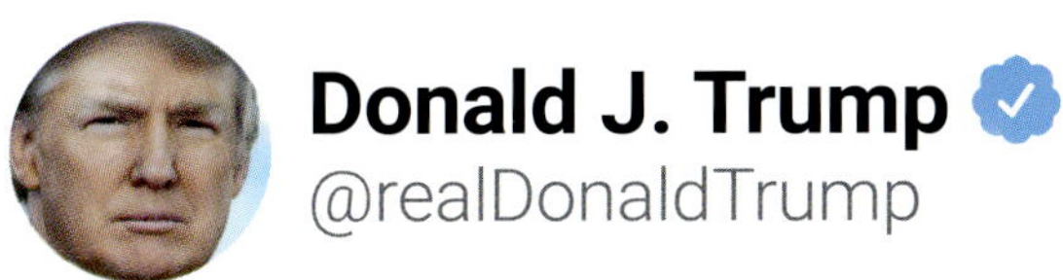

Donald J. Trump ✔
@realDonaldTrump

Sometimes by losing a battle you find a new way to win the war. Don't ever get down on yourself, just keep fighting - in the end, you WIN!

8:27 AM · May 23, 2014

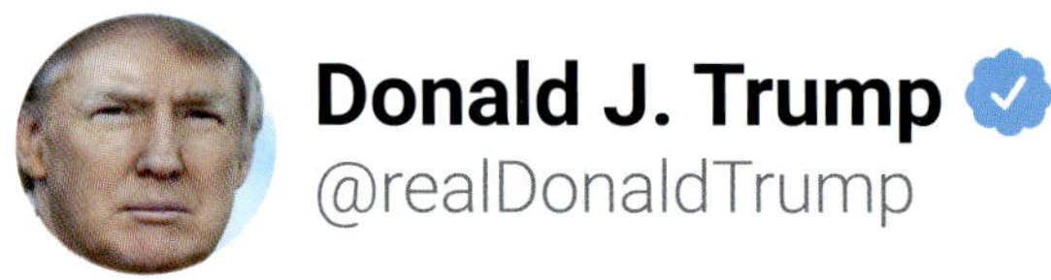

"May God have mercy upon my enemies, because I won't"
--General George S. Patton

11:45 PM · Jun 18, 2014

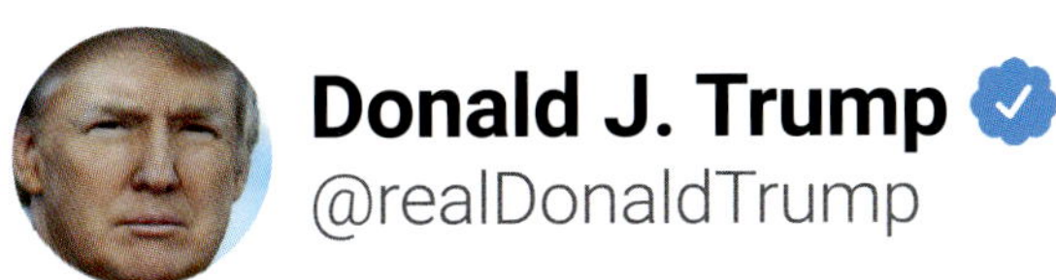

If Obama resigns from office NOW, thereby doing a great service to the country—I will give him free lifetime golf at any one of my courses!

5:22 PM · Sep 10, 2014

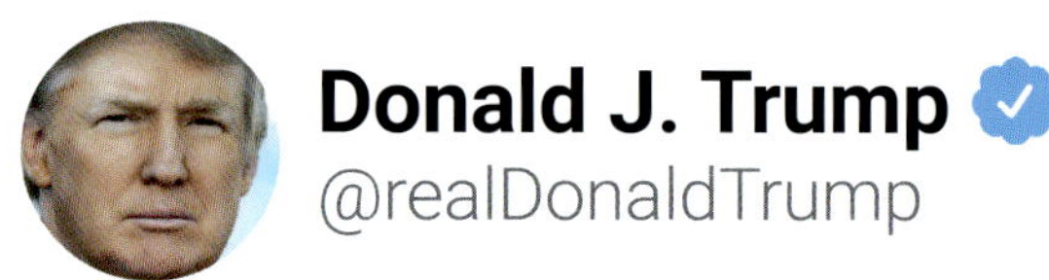

Donald J. Trump ✔
@realDonaldTrump

Every time I speak of the haters and losers I do so with great love and affection. They cannot help the fact that they were born fucked up!

8:21 PM · Sep 28, 2014

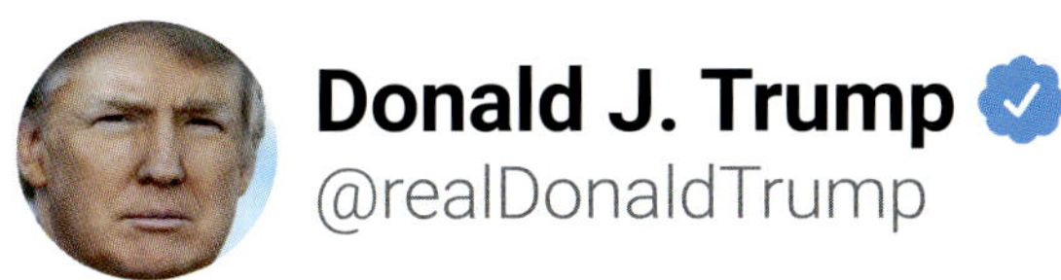

Deals are my art form. Other people paint beautifully or write poetry. I like making deals, preferably big deals. That's how I get my kicks.

10:39 AM · Dec 29, 2014

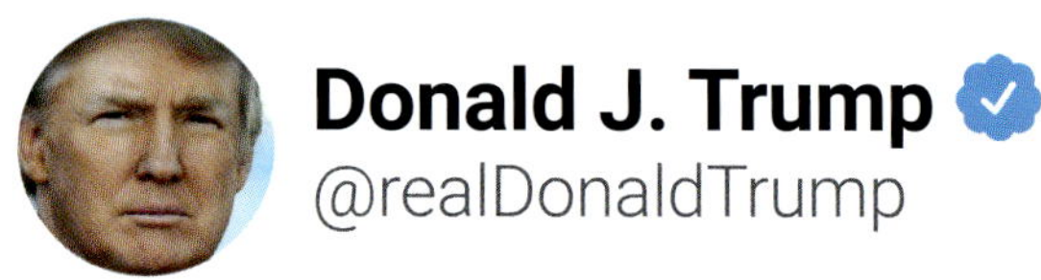

Donald J. Trump
@realDonaldTrump
"When you can't make them see the light, make them feel the heat." – Ronald Reagan
2:43 PM • Apr 21, 2015

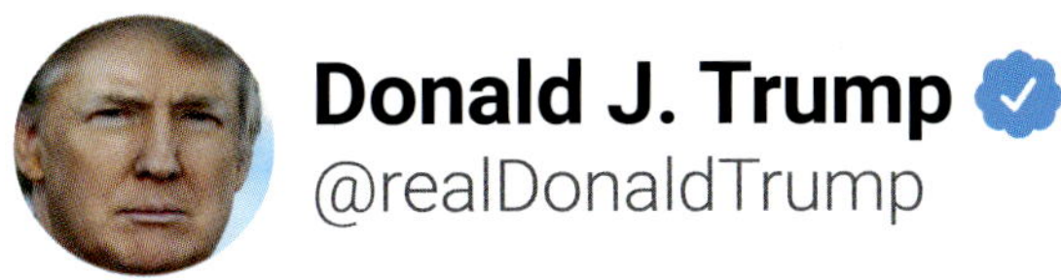

Donald J. Trump ✔
@realDonaldTrump

I am officially running for President of the United States.
#MakeAmericaGreatAgain

11:57 AM · Jun 16, 2015

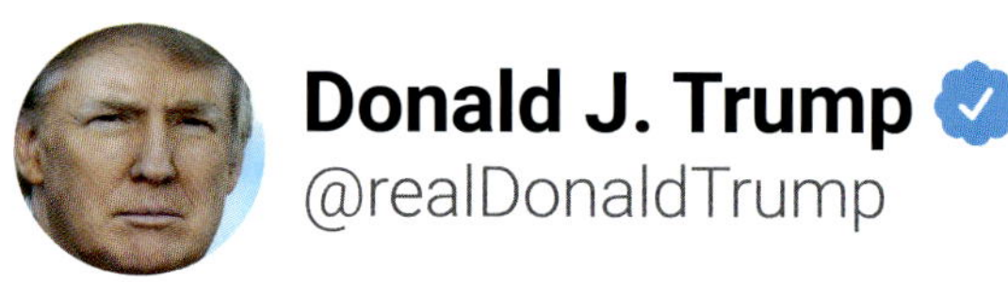

Donald J. Trump
@realDonaldTrump

When somebody challenges you unfairly, fight back - be brutal, be tough - don't take it. It is always important to WIN!

10:50 AM • Jun 27, 2015

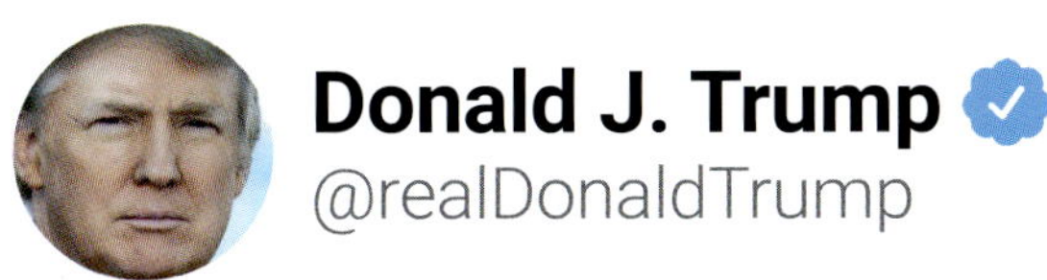

So many "politically correct" fools in our country. We have to all get back to work and stop wasting time and energy on nonsense!

8:29 AM • Aug 8, 2015

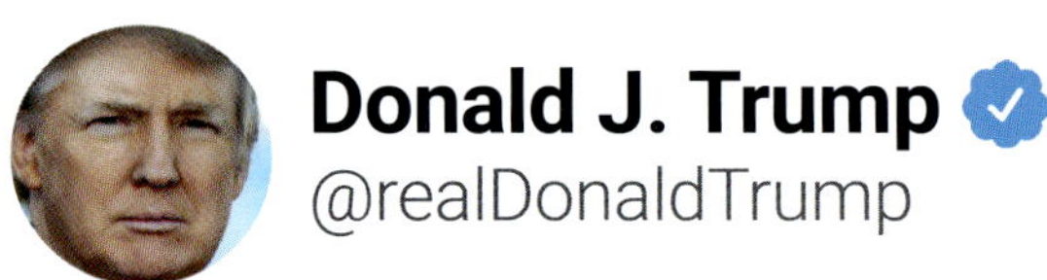

For those that don't think a wall (fence) works, why don't they suggest taking down the fence around the White House? Foolish people!

11:05 AM · Aug 31, 2015

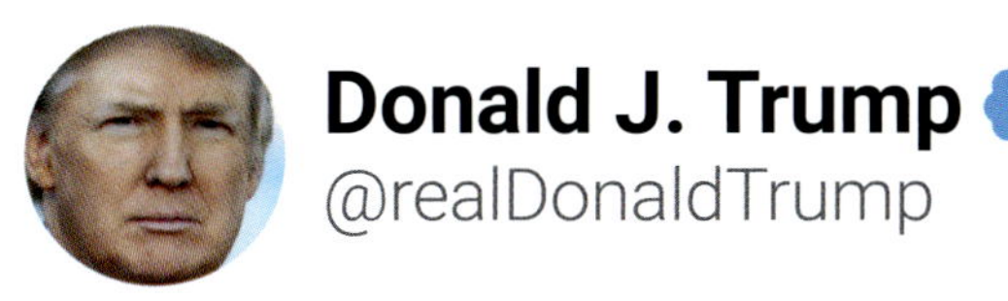

Donald J. Trump
@realDonaldTrump
By self-funding my campaign, I am not controlled by my donors, special interests or lobbyists. I am only working for the people of the U.S.!
5:50 PM · Sep 5, 2015

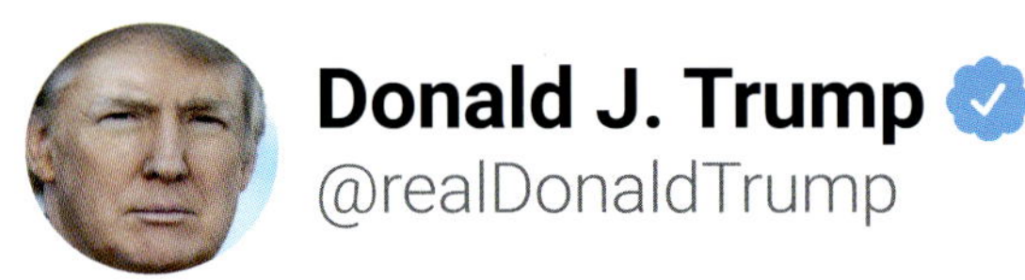
Donald J. Trump
@realDonaldTrump
This is the first time in my life that I have caused controversy
by NOT saying something.
8:52 AM · Sep 19, 2015

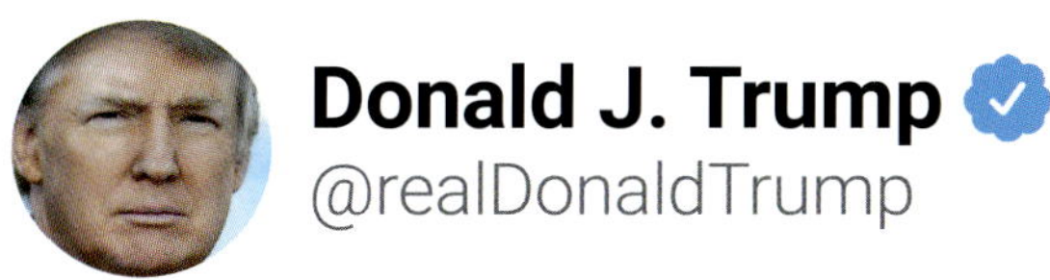

We, as a country, either have borders or we don't. IF WE DON'T HAVE BORDERS, WE DON'T HAVE A COUNTRY!

7:50 AM • Nov 12, 2015

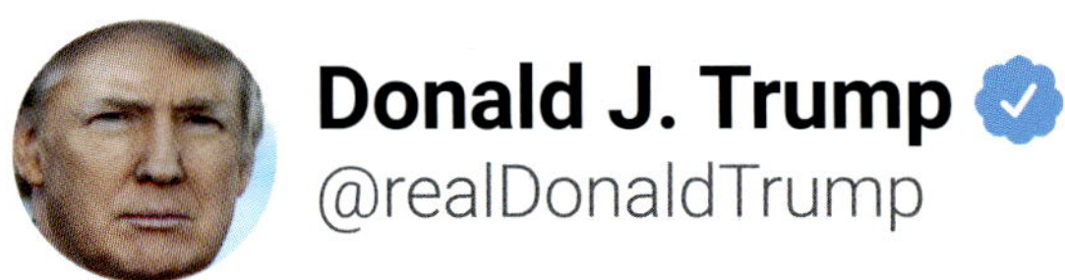

Donald J. Trump
@realDonaldTrump
Dopey Prince @Alwaleed_Talal wants to control our U.S. politicians with daddy's money. Can't do it when I get elected. #Trump2016
10:53 PM • Dec 11, 2015

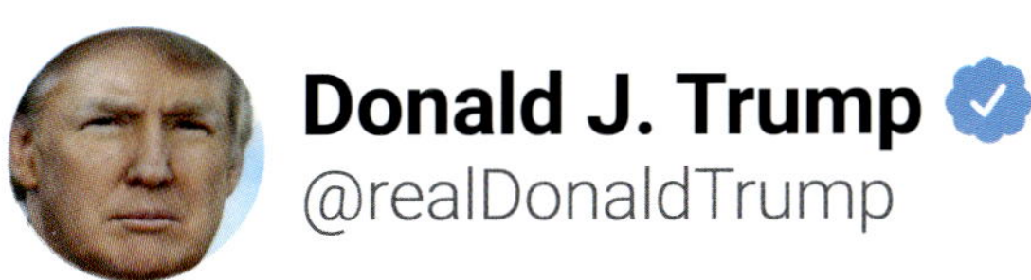

When I said that Hillary Clinton got schlonged by Obama, it meant got beaten badly. The media knows this. Often used word in politics!

10:37 PM · Dec 22, 2015

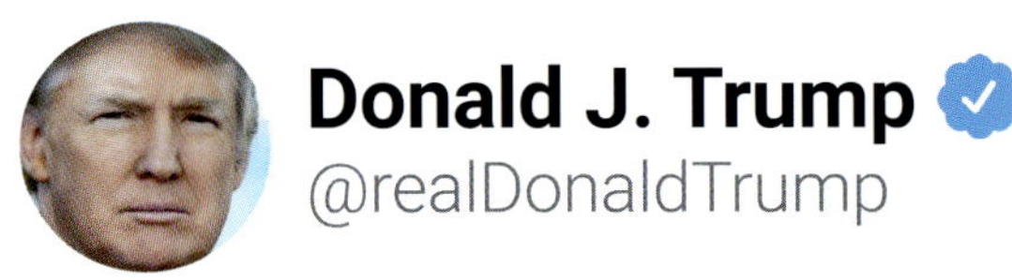

Donald J. Trump
@realDonaldTrump

Hillary said "I really deplore the tone and inflammatory rhetoric
of his campaign." I deplore the death and destruction she
caused-stupidity

10:22 PM · Dec 23, 2015

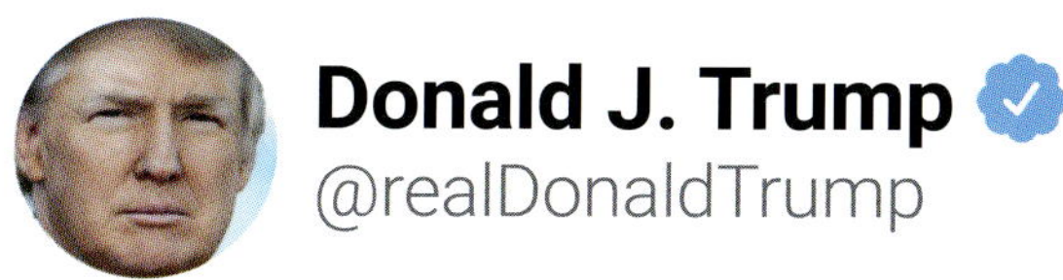

Donald J. Trump
@realDonaldTrump

If Hillary thinks she can unleash her husband, with his terrible
record of women abuse, while playing the women's card on
me, she's wrong!

7:12 AM · Dec 28, 2015

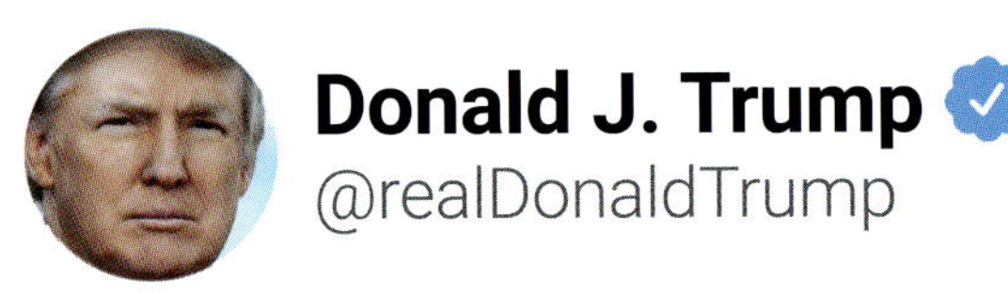
Donald J. Trump
@realDonaldTrump
I refuse to call Megyn Kelly a bimbo, because that would not be politically correct. Instead I will only call her a lightweight reporter!
6:44 AM • Jan 27, 2016

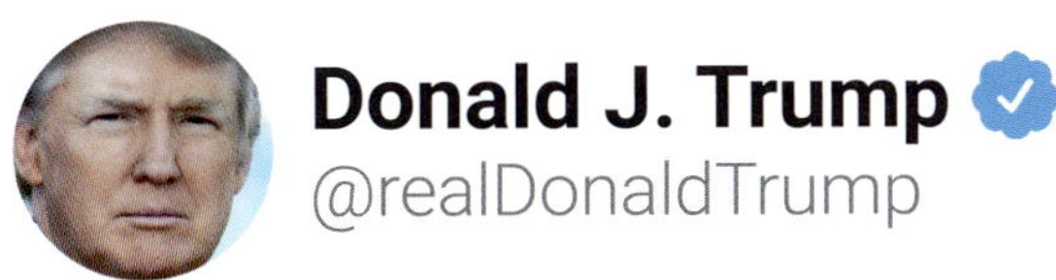

Donald J. Trump ✓
@realDonaldTrump

After today, Crooked Hillary can officially be called Lyin'
Crooked Hillary.

9:52 PM • Jul 7, 2016

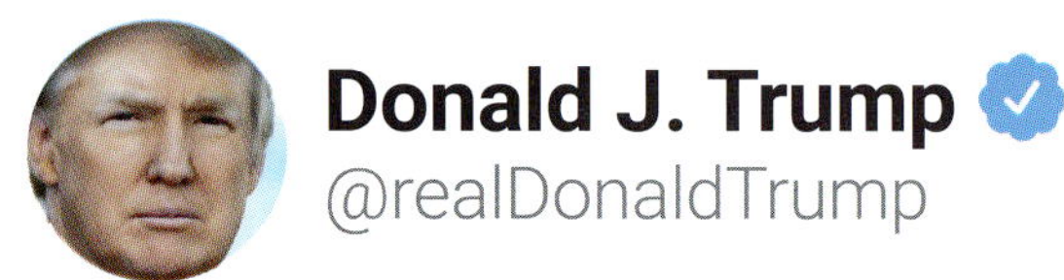

The media is so dishonest. If I make a statement, they twist it and turn it to make it sound bad or foolish.They think the public is stupid!

2:42 PM · Jul 10, 2016

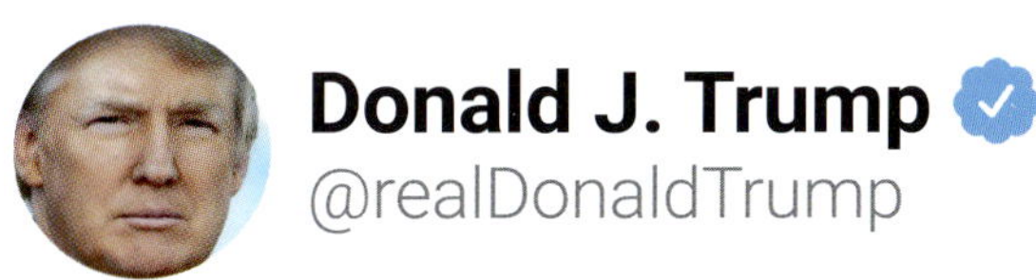

Wow, President Obama's brother, Malik, just announced that he is voting for me. Was probably treated badly by president-like everybody else!

7:56 AM • Jul 24, 2016

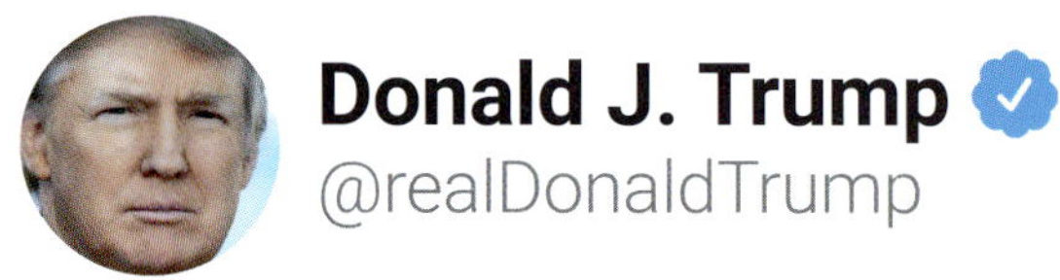

Not one American flag on the massive stage at the Democratic National Convention until people started complaining-then a small one. Pathetic

9:01 AM · Jul 27, 2016

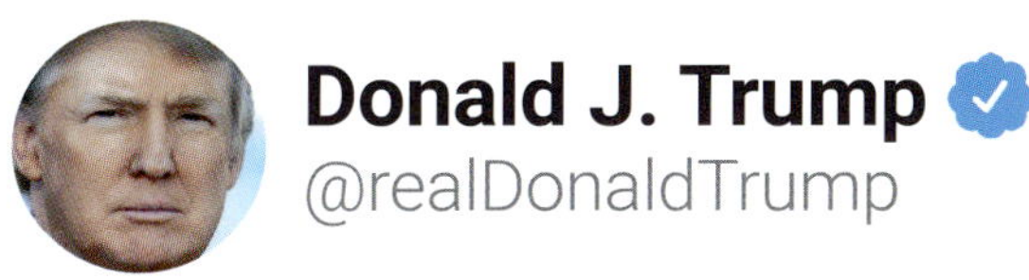

President Obama will go down as perhaps the worst president in the history of the United States!

3:07 PM • Aug 2, 2016

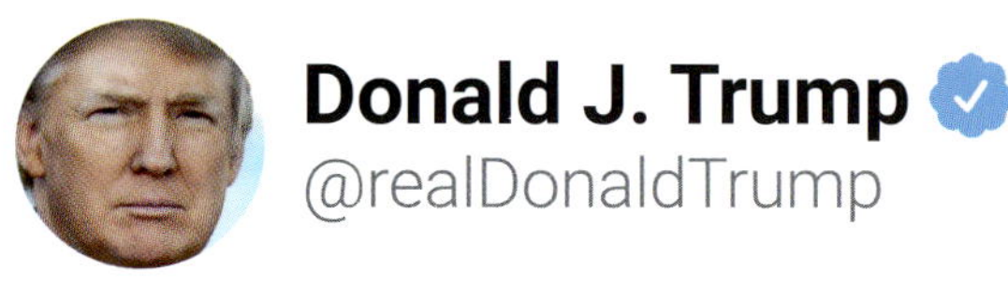

Donald J. Trump
@realDonaldTrump
Mexico will pay for the wall!
6:31 AM · Sep 1, 2016

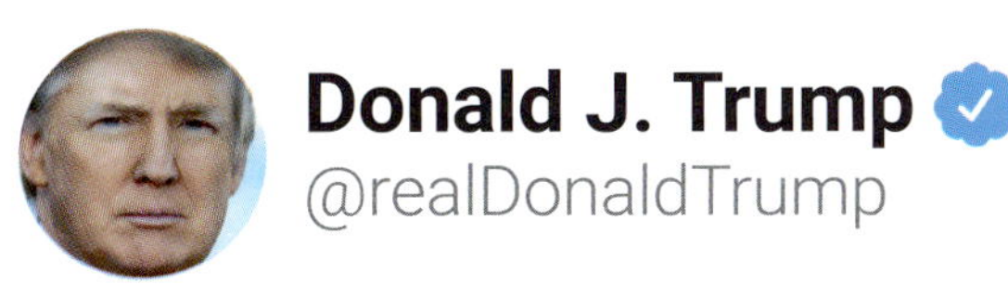

For those few people knocking me for tweeting at three o'clock in the morning, at least you know I will be there, awake, to answer the call!

2:37 PM · Sep 30, 2016

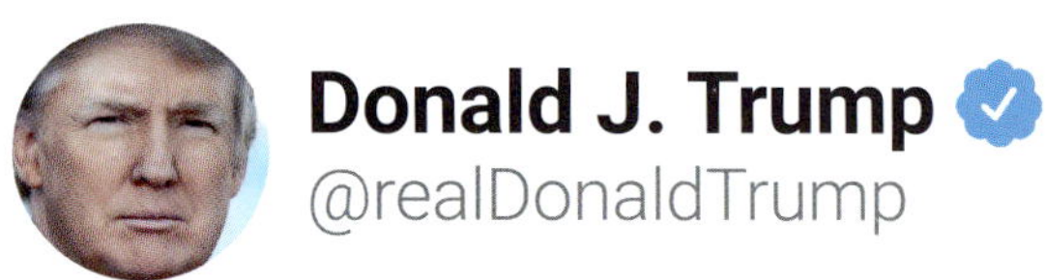

Disloyal R's are far more difficult than Crooked Hillary.
They come at you from all sides. They don't know how to win -
I will teach them!

10:48 AM · Oct 11, 2016

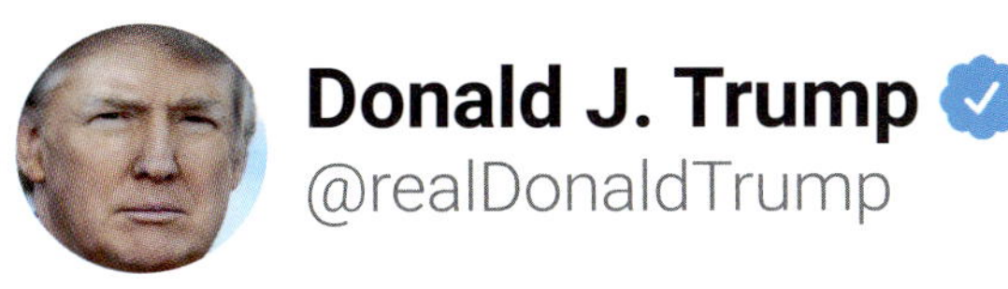

Donald J. Trump
@realDonaldTrump

TODAY WE MAKE AMERICA GREAT AGAIN!

6:43 AM • Nov 8, 2016

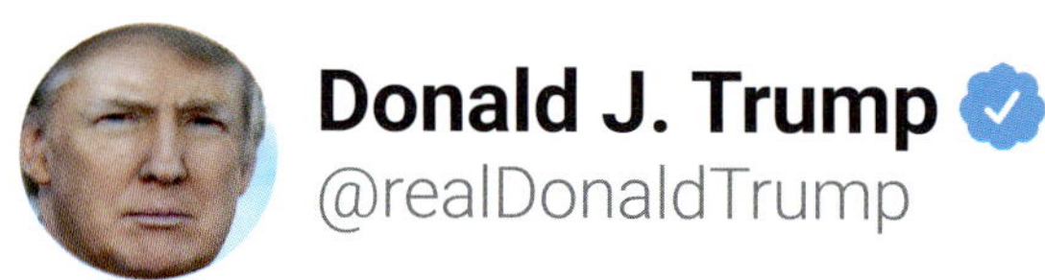

Donald J. Trump
@realDonaldTrump
Such a beautiful and important evening! The forgotten man and woman will never be forgotten again. We will all come together as never before
6:36 AM • Nov 9, 2016

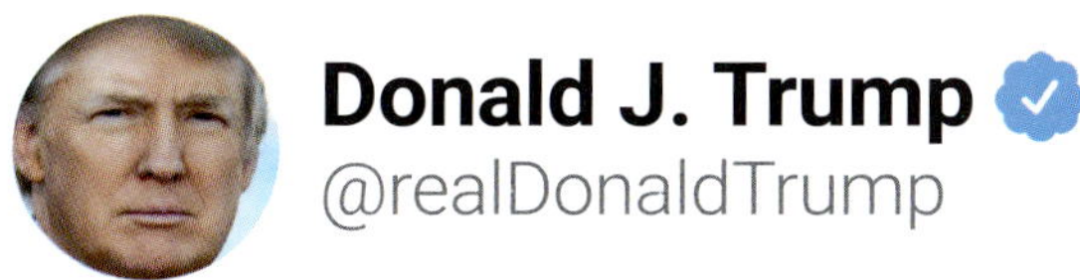

Fidel Castro is dead!

8:08 AM · Nov 26, 2016

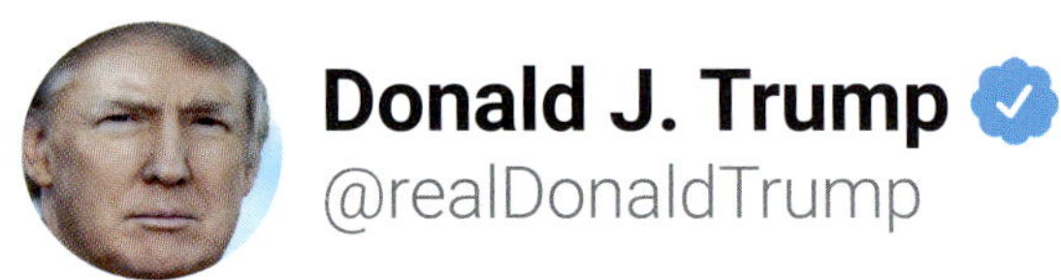

Donald J. Trump ✔
@realDonaldTrump

Nobody should be allowed to burn the American flag - if they do, there must be consequences - perhaps loss of citizenship or year in jail!

6:55 AM · Nov 29, 2016

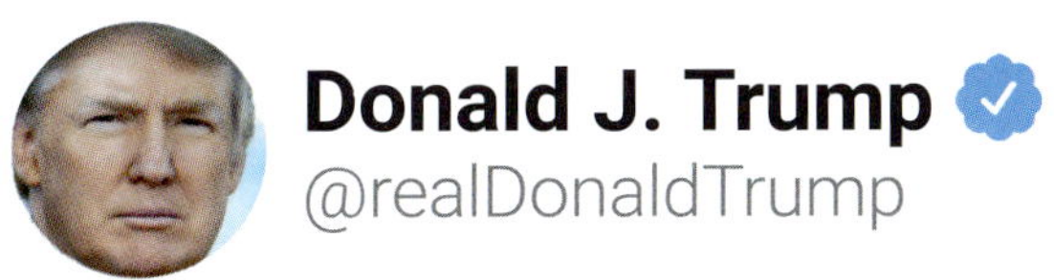

Donald J. Trump
@realDonaldTrump
If the press would cover me accurately & honorably, I would have far less reason to "tweet." Sadly, I don't know if that will ever happen!
11:00 AM · Dec 5, 2016

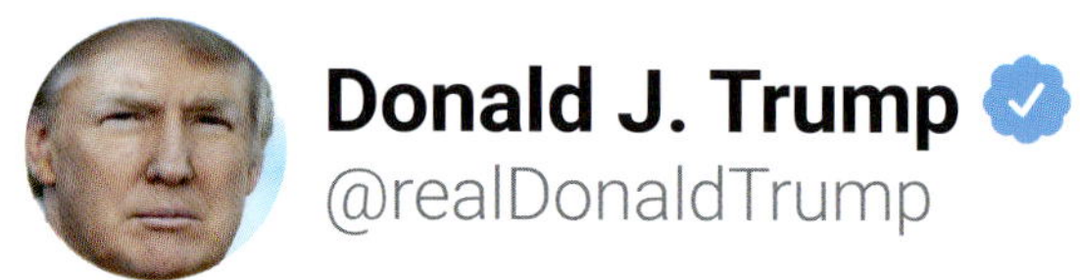

Donald J. Trump @realDonaldTrump

The so-called "A" list celebrities are all wanting tixs to the inauguration, but look what they did for Hillary, NOTHING. I want the PEOPLE!

8:59 PM · Dec 22, 2016

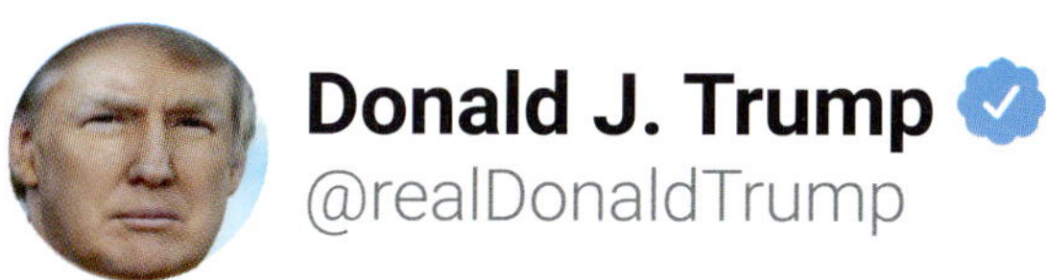

Donald J. Trump ✔
@realDonaldTrump

Happy New Year to all, including to my many enemies and those who have fought me and lost so badly they just don't know what to do. Love!

8:17 AM · Dec 31, 2016

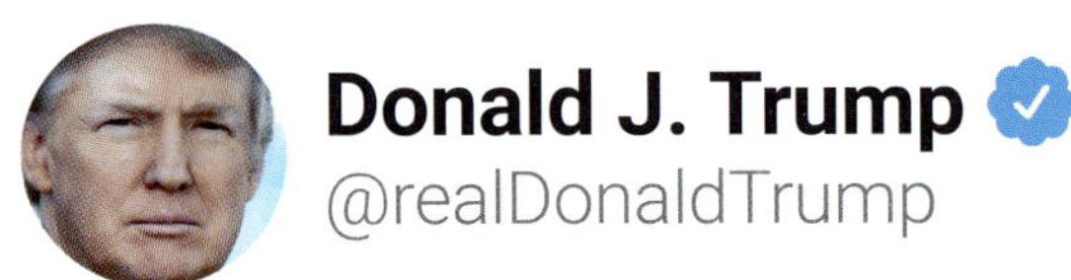
Donald J. Trump
@realDonaldTrump
What truly matters is not which party controls our government, but whether our government is controlled by the people.
12:52 PM • Jan 20, 2017

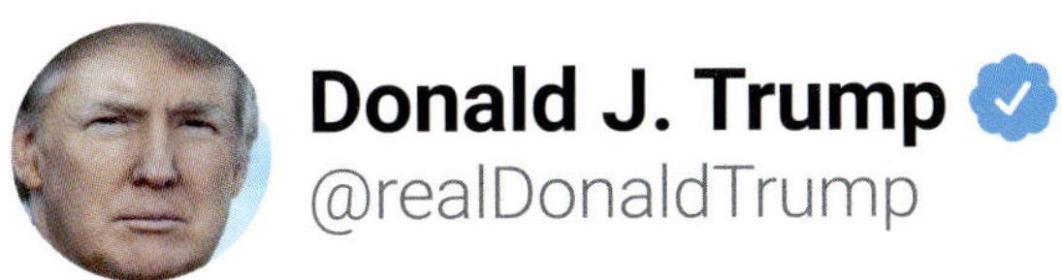

Donald J. Trump
@realDonaldTrump
The forgotten men and women of our country will be forgotten no longer. From this moment on, it's going to be #AmericaFirst 🇺🇸
12:54 PM · Jan 20, 2017

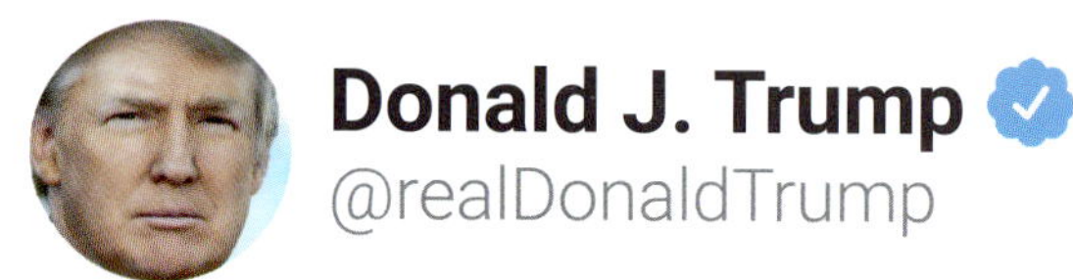

Donald J. Trump ✔
@realDonaldTrump

We will follow two simple rules: BUY AMERICAN &
HIRE AMERICAN!
#InaugurationDay #MAGA 🇺🇸

12:55 PM · Jan 20, 2017

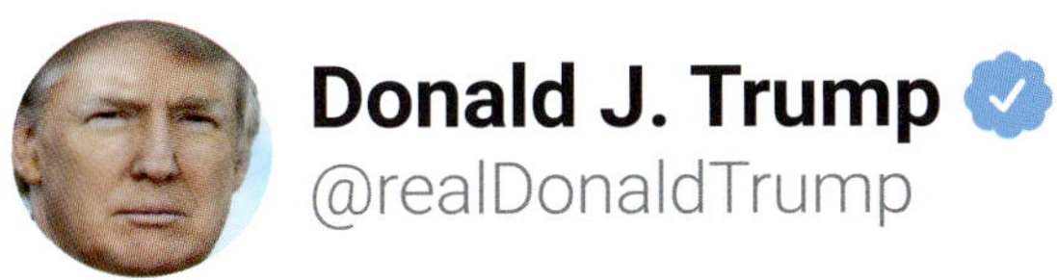

The #MarchForLife is so important. To all of you marching --- you have my full support!

11:27 AM · Jan 27, 2017

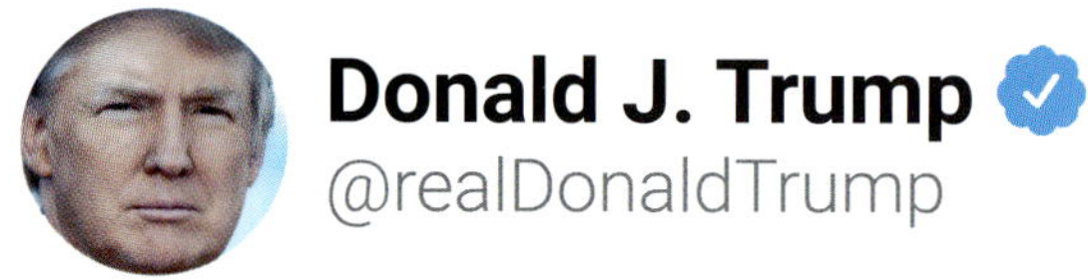

Donald J. Trump
@realDonaldTrump
We must keep "evil" out of our country!
6:08 PM · Feb 3, 2017

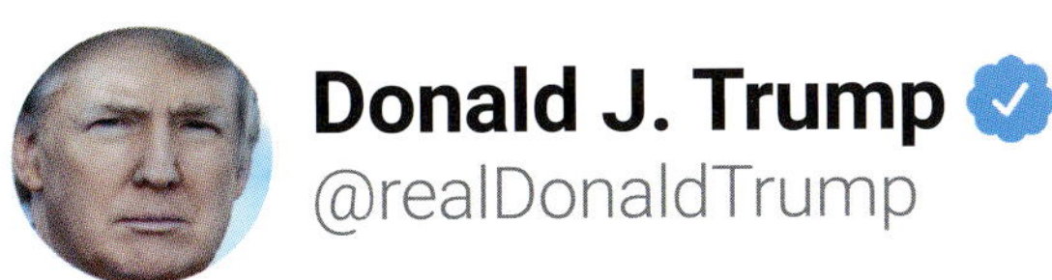

Donald J. Trump ✔
@realDonaldTrump

I don't know Putin, have no deals in Russia, and the haters
are going crazy - yet Obama can make a deal with Iran,
#1 in terror, no problem!

7:11 AM • Feb 7, 2017

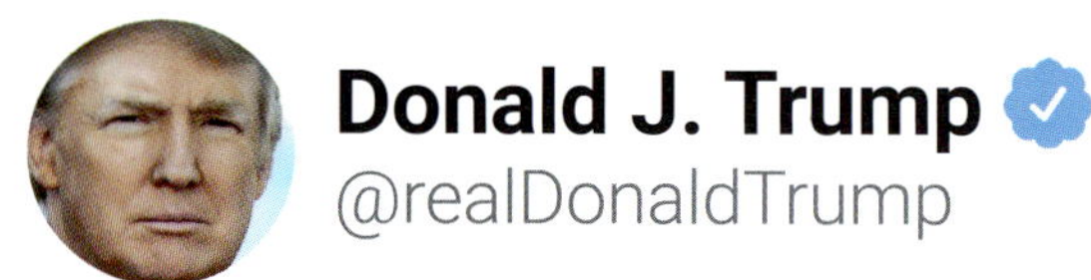

The FAKE NEWS media (failing @nytimes, @NBCNews, @ABC, @CBS, @CNN) is not my enemy, it is the enemy of the American People!

4:48 PM · Feb 17, 2017

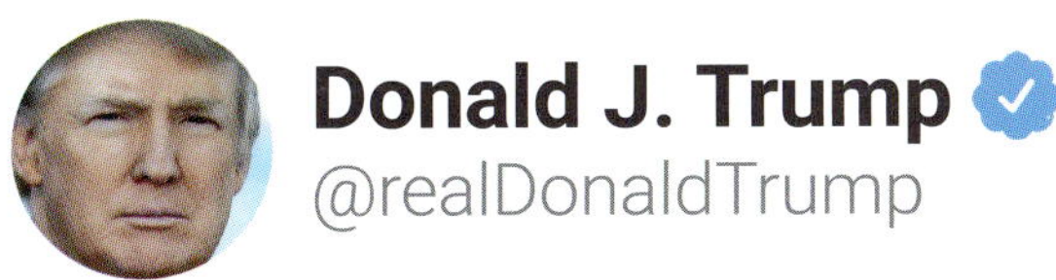

Donald J. Trump ✔
@realDonaldTrump

How low has President Obama gone to tapp my phones during the very sacred election process. This is Nixon/Watergate. Bad (or sick) guy!

7:02 AM • Mar 4, 2017

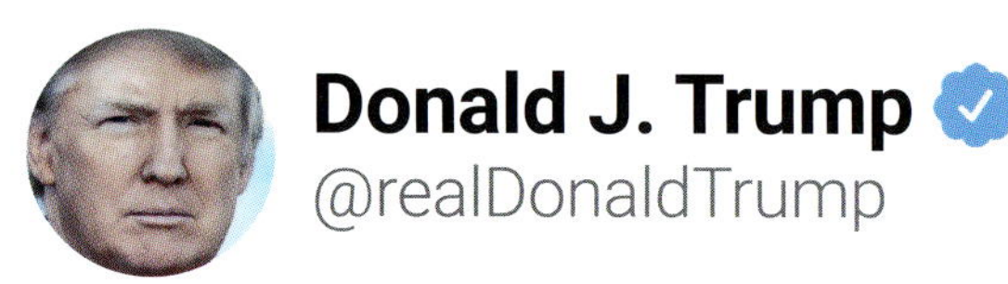

Donald J. Trump ✔
@realDonaldTrump

The Fake News Media works hard at disparaging &
demeaning my use of social media because they don't want
America to hear the real story!

8:20 PM • May 28, 2017

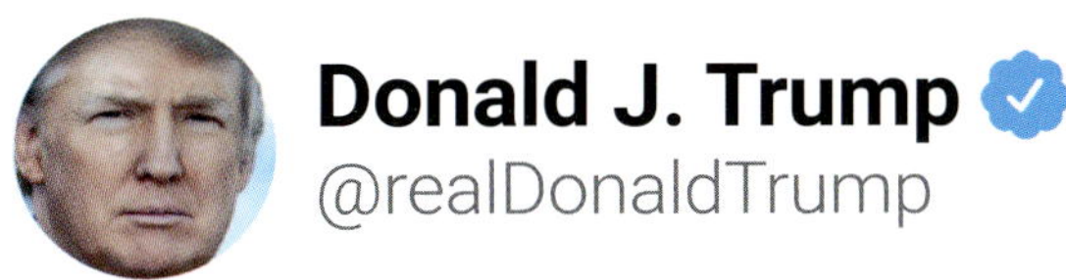

Donald J. Trump
@realDonaldTrump

Despite the constant negative press covfefe

12:06 AM · May 31, 2017

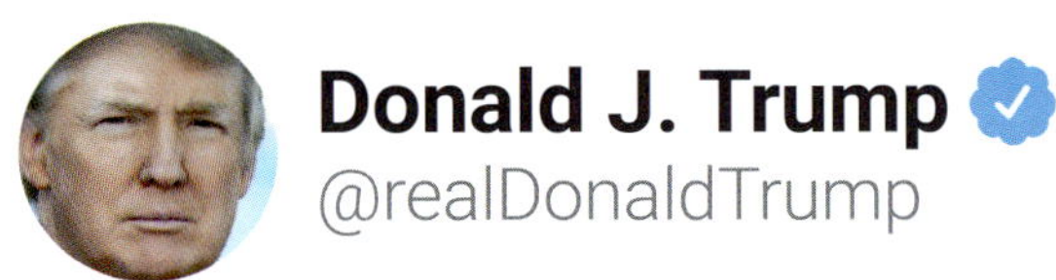

Donald J. Trump ✓
@realDonaldTrump

My use of social media is not Presidential - it's MODERN DAY PRESIDENTIAL. Make America Great Again!

6:41 PM · Jul 1, 2017

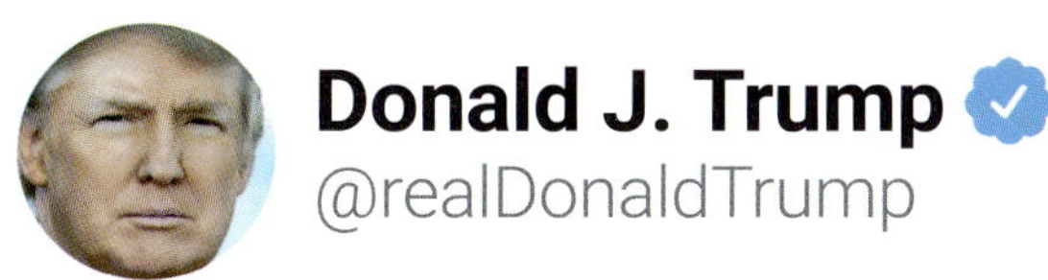

Donald J. Trump ✔
@realDonaldTrump

It's very sad that Republicans, even some that were carried over the line on my back, do very little to protect their President.

4:14 PM · Jul 23, 2017

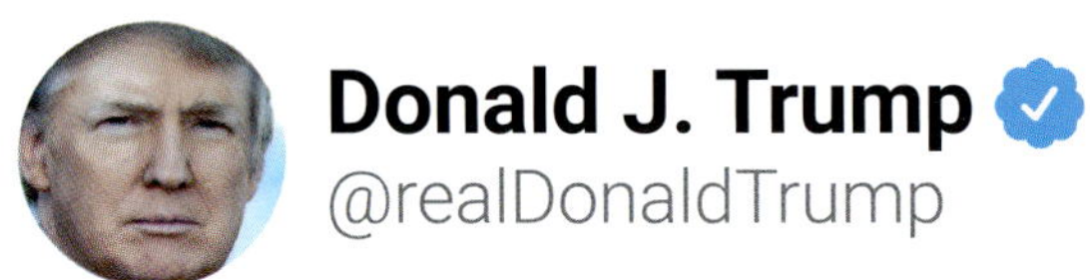

Drain the Swamp should be changed to Drain the Sewer - it's actually much worse than anyone ever thought, and it begins with the Fake News!

6:40 AM • Jul 24, 2017

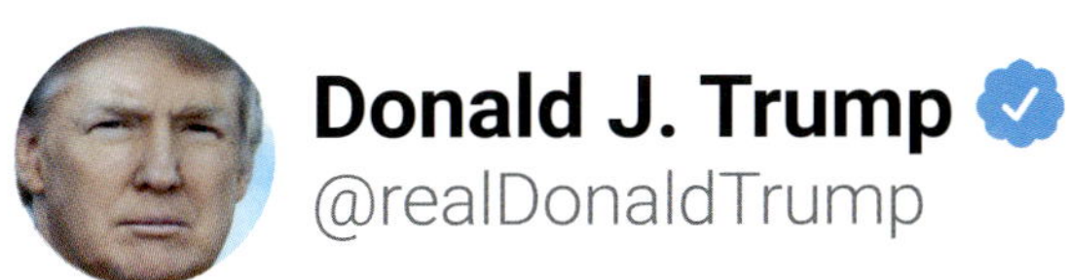

Only the Fake News Media and Trump enemies want me to stop using Social Media (110 million people). Only way for me to get the truth out!

9:55 AM · Aug 1, 2017

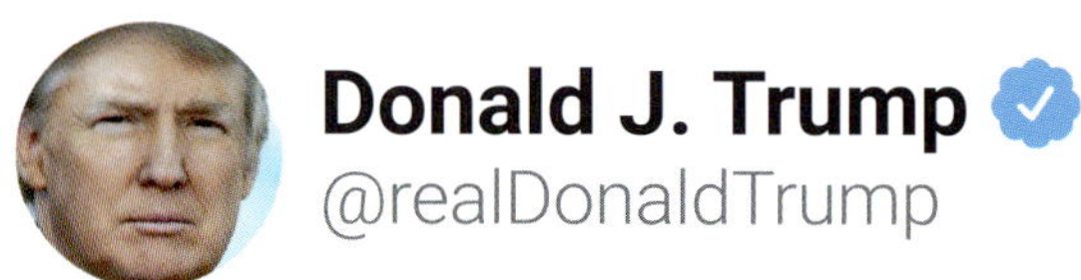

We ALL must be united & condemn all that hate stands for. There is no place for this kind of violence in America. Lets come together as one!

1:19 PM • Aug 12, 2017

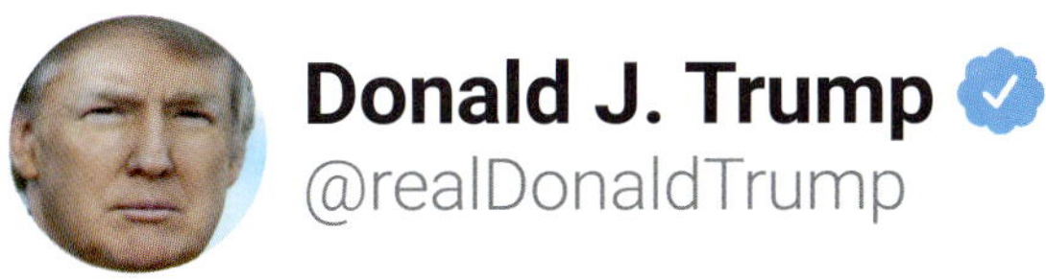

We must remember this truth: No matter our color, creed, religion or political party, we are ALL AMERICANS FIRST.

5:19 PM · Aug 12, 2017

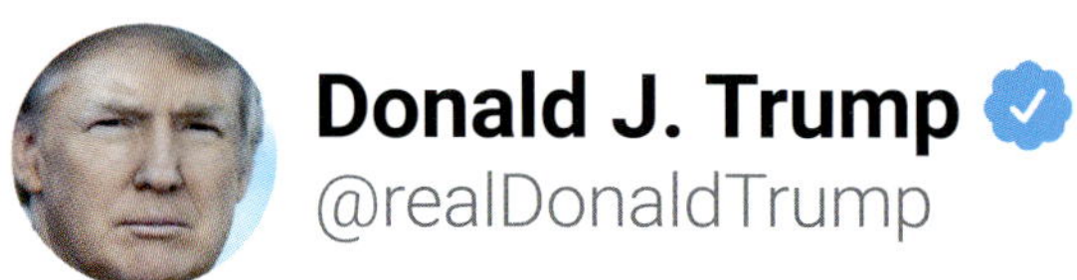

Donald J. Trump
@realDonaldTrump
Crooked Hillary Clinton blames everybody (and every thing) but herself for her election loss. She lost the debates and lost her direction!
10:47 PM · Sep 13, 2017

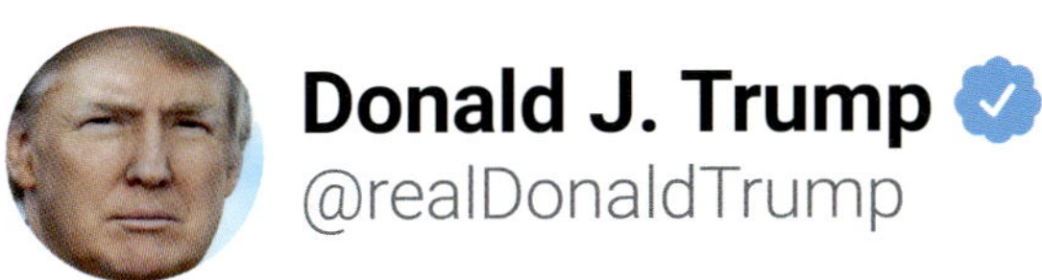

Donald J. Trump
@realDonaldTrump

Courageous Patriots have fought and died for our great American Flag --- we MUST honor and respect it! MAKE AMERICA GREAT AGAIN!

3:32 PM · Sep 24, 2017

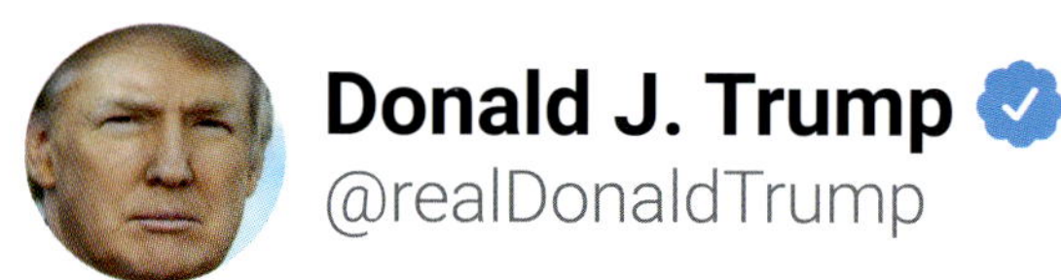

Donald J. Trump
@realDonaldTrump
The issue of kneeling has nothing to do with race. It is about respect for our Country, Flag and National Anthem. NFL must respect this!
7:39 AM · Sep 25, 2017

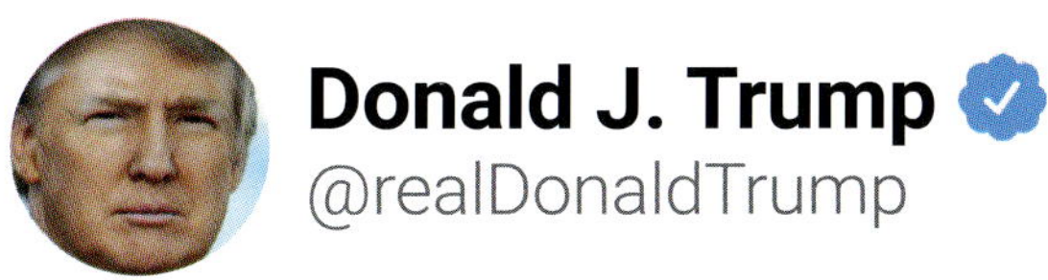

Donald J. Trump
@realDonaldTrump
#StandForOurAnthem
9:02 AM · Sep 25, 2017

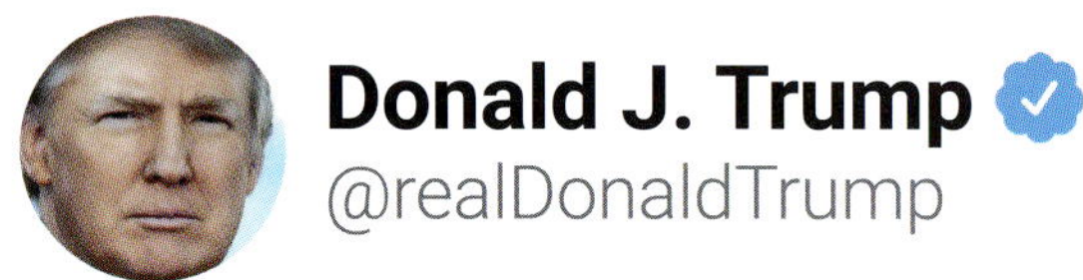

Donald J. Trump
@realDonaldTrump

Being nice to Rocket Man hasn't worked in 25 years, why would it work now? Clinton failed, Bush failed, and Obama failed. I won't fail.

3:01 PM · Oct 1, 2017

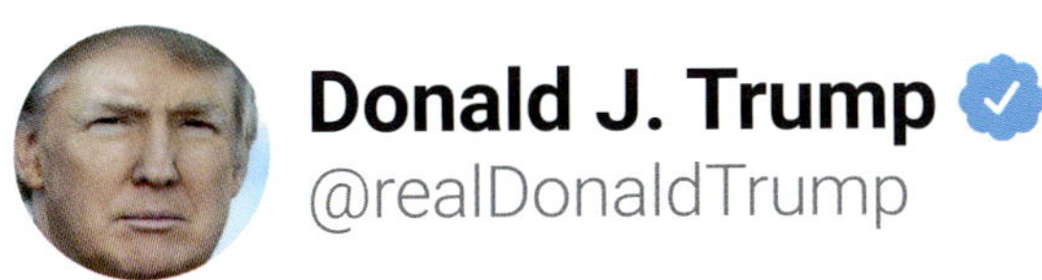

Donald J. Trump
@realDonaldTrump

My Twitter account was taken down for 11 minutes by a
rogue employee. I guess the word must finally be getting
out-and having an impact.

6:51 AM · Nov 3, 2017

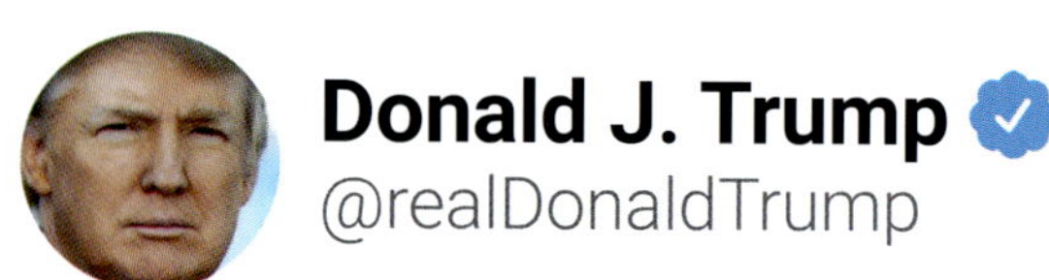

When will all the haters and fools out there realize that having a good relationship with Russia is a good thing, not a bad thing. There always playing politics - bad for our country. I want to solve North Korea, Syria, Ukraine, terrorism, and Russia can greatly help!

7:18 PM • Nov 11, 2017

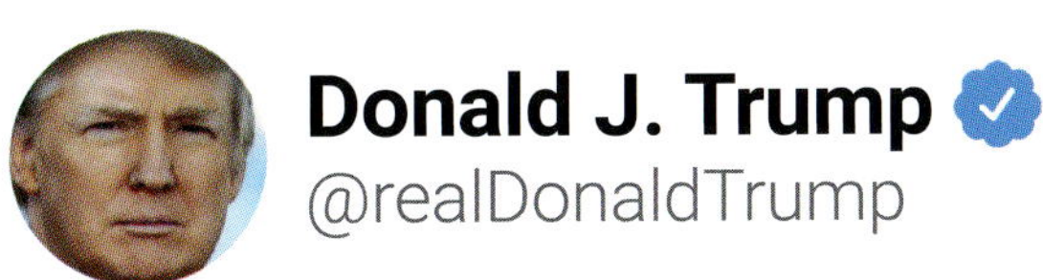

Donald J. Trump ✓
@realDonaldTrump

Why would Kim Jong-un insult me by calling me "old," when I would NEVER call him "short and fat?" Oh well, I try so hard to be his friend - and maybe someday that will happen!

7:48 PM • Nov 11, 2017

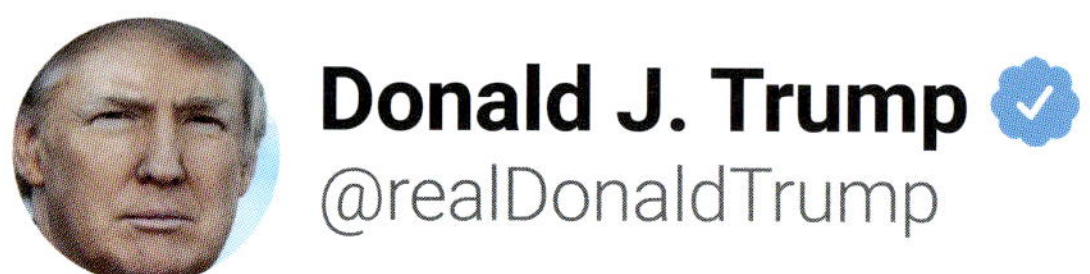

Donald J. Trump ✓
@realDonaldTrump

Crooked Hillary Clinton is the worst (and biggest) loser of all time. She just can't stop, which is so good for the Republican Party. Hillary, get on with your life and give it another try in three years!

8:31 AM • Nov 18, 2017

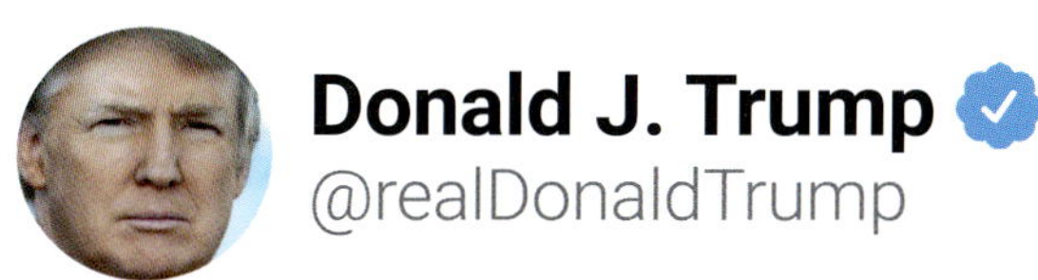

Donald J. Trump
@realDonaldTrump

Since the first day I took office, all you hear is the phony
Democrat excuse for losing the election, Russia, Russia,
Russia. Despite this I have the economy booming and
have possibly done more than any 10 month President.
MAKE AMERICA GREAT AGAIN!

4:29 PM · Nov 26, 2017

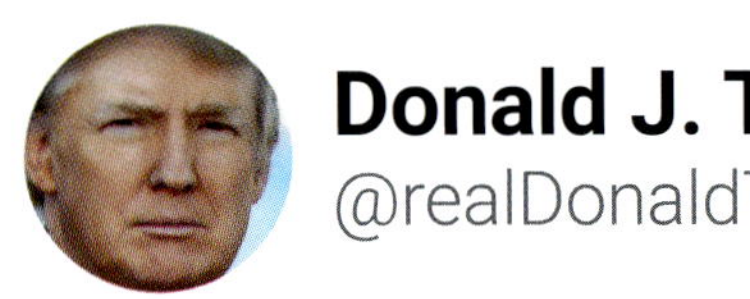
Donald J. Trump
@realDonaldTrump

People are proud to be saying Merry Christmas again. I am proud to have led the charge against the assault of our cherished and beautiful phrase. MERRY CHRISTMAS!!!!!

9:56 PM · Dec 24, 2017

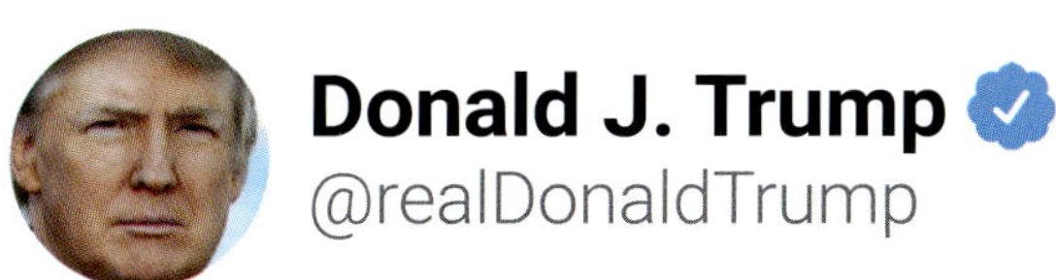

I use Social Media not because I like to, but because it is the only way to fight a VERY dishonest and unfair "press," now often referred to as Fake News Media. Phony and non-existent "sources" are being used more often than ever. Many stories & reports a pure fiction!

5:36 PM · Dec 30, 2017

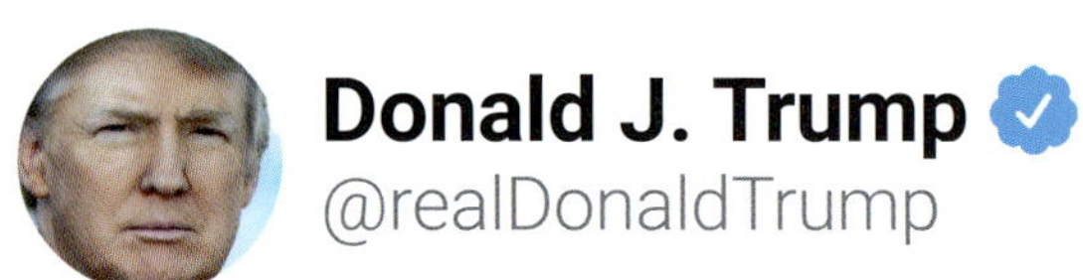

North Korean Leader Kim Jong Un just stated that the "Nuclear Button is on his desk at all times." Will someone from his depleted and food starved regime please inform him that I too have a Nuclear Button, but it is a much bigger & more powerful one than his, and my Button works!

7:49 PM · Jan 2, 2018

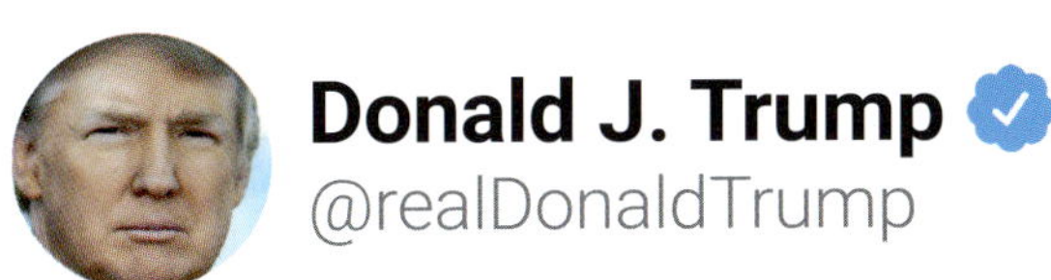

Now that Russian collusion, after one year of intense study, has proven to be a total hoax on the American public, the Democrats and their lapdogs, the Fake News Mainstream Media, are taking out the old Ronald Reagan playbook and screaming mental stability and intelligence. Actually, throughout my life, my two greatest assets have been mental stability and being, like, really smart. Crooked Hillary Clinton also played these cards very hard and, as everyone knows, went down in flames. I went from VERY successful businessman, to top T.V. Star to President of the United States (on my first try). I think that would qualify as not smart, but genius....and a very stable genius at that!

7:19 AM · Jan 6, 2018

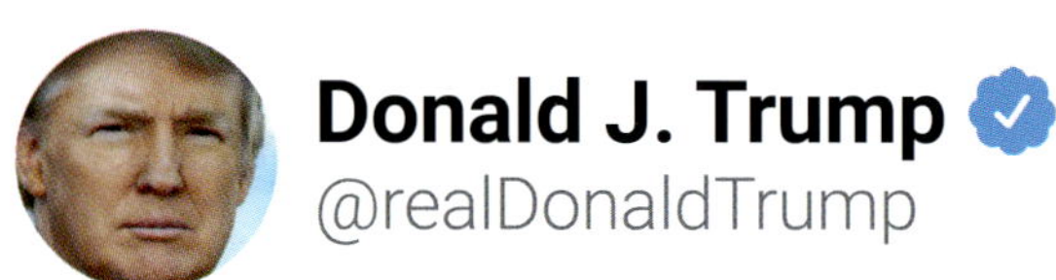

When a country (USA) is losing many billions of dollars on trade with virtually every country it does business with, trade wars are good, and easy to win. Example, when we are down $100 billion with a certain country and they get cute, don't trade anymore-we win big. It's easy!

5:50 AM · Mar 2, 2018

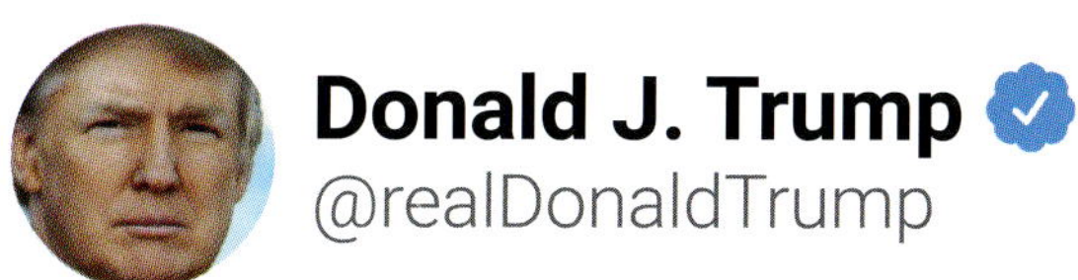

Donald J. Trump ✔
@realDonaldTrump

THE HOUSE INTELLIGENCE COMMITTEE HAS, AFTER A 14 MONTH LONG IN-DEPTH INVESTIGATION, FOUND NO EVIDENCE OF COLLUSION OR COORDINATION BETWEEN THE TRUMP CAMPAIGN AND RUSSIA TO INFLUENCE THE 2016 PRESIDENTIAL ELECTION.

8:49 PM · Mar 12, 2018

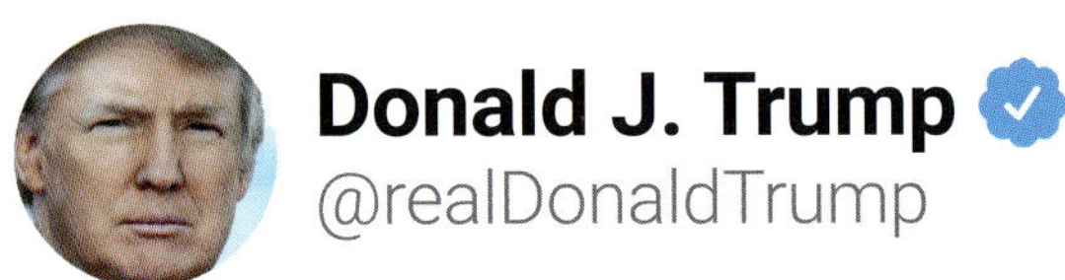

Crazy Joe Biden is trying to act like a tough guy. Actually, he is weak, both mentally and physically, and yet he threatens me, for the second time, with physical assault. He doesn't know me, but he would go down fast and hard, crying all the way. Don't threaten people Joe!

6:19 AM • Mar 22, 2018

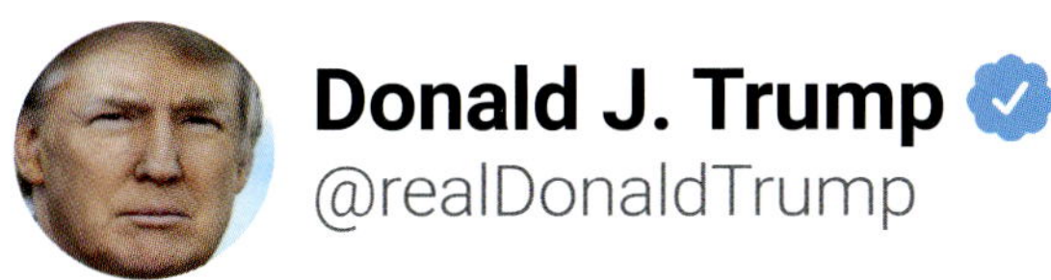

Donald J. Trump
@realDonaldTrump
Thank you Kanye, very cool!
KANYE WEST @kanyewest
You don't have to agree with trump but the mob can't make me not love him. We are both dragon energy. He is my brother. I love everyone. I don't agree with everything anyone does. That's what makes us individuals. And we have the right to independent thought.
3:33 PM · Apr 25, 2018

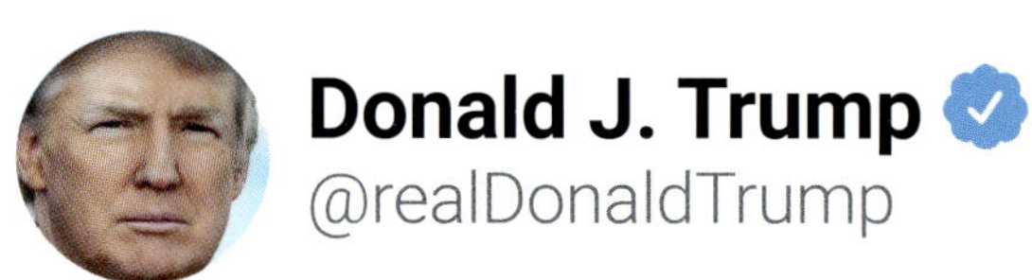

Donald J. Trump ✔
@realDonaldTrump

Happy Memorial Day! Those who died for our great country would be very happy and proud at how well our country is doing today. Best economy in decades, lowest unemployment numbers for Blacks and Hispanics EVER (& women in 18years), rebuilding our Military and so much more. Nice!

8:58 AM • May 28, 2018

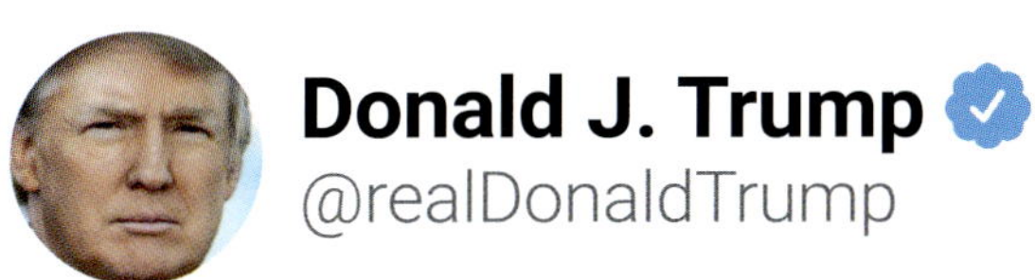

Donald J. Trump ✔
@realDonaldTrump

My supporters are the smartest, strongest, most hard working and most loyal that we have seen in our countries history. It is a beautiful thing to watch as we win elections and gather support from all over the country. As we get stronger, so does our country. Best numbers ever!

9:12 AM • Jun 16, 2018

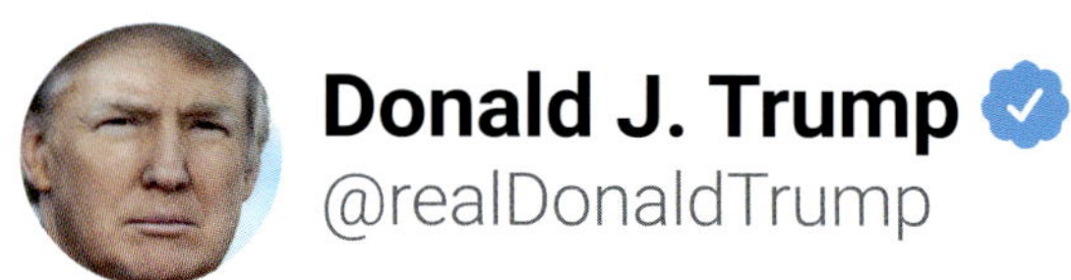

Donald J. Trump ✓
@realDonaldTrump

Democrats are the problem. They don't care about crime and want illegal immigrants, no matter how bad they may be, to pour into and infest our Country, like MS-13. They can't win on their terrible policies, so they view them as potential voters!

9:52 AM • Jun 19, 2018

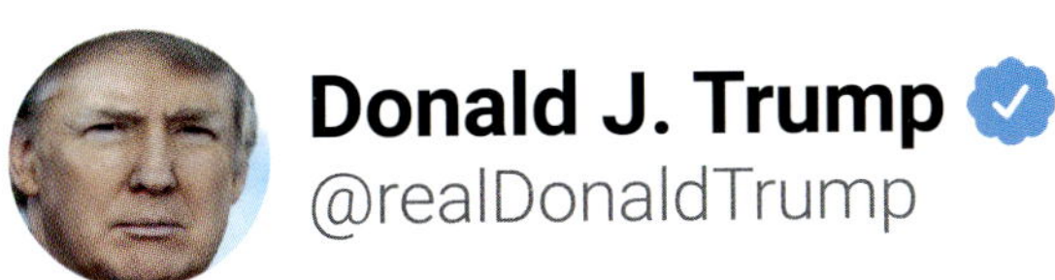

After having written many best selling books, and somewhat priding myself on my ability to write, it should be noted that the Fake News constantly likes to pore over my tweets looking for a mistake. I capitalize certain words only for emphasis, not b/c they should be capitalized!

7:13 PM • Jul 3, 2018

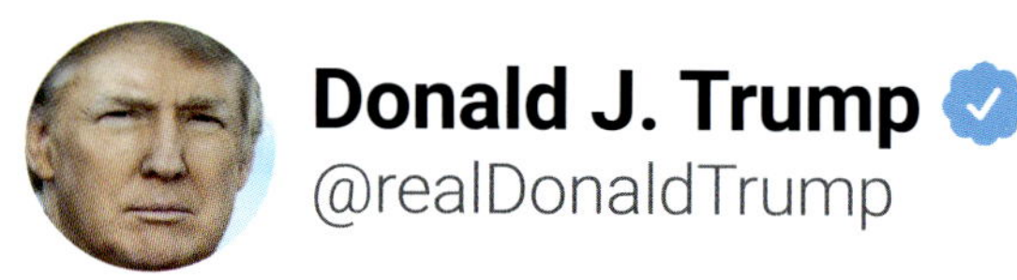

Some people HATE the fact that I got along well with President Putin of Russia. They would rather go to war than see this. It's called Trump Derangement Syndrome!

7:27 AM • Jul 18, 2018

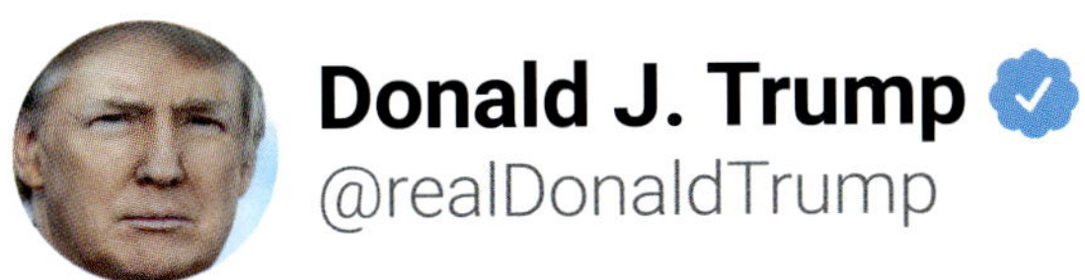

To Iranian President Rouhani: NEVER, EVER THREATEN THE UNITED STATES AGAIN OR YOU WILL SUFFER CONSEQUENCES THE LIKES OF WHICH FEW THROUGHOUT HISTORY HAVE EVER SUFFERED BEFORE. WE ARE NO LONGER A COUNTRY THAT WILL STAND FOR YOUR DEMENTED WORDS OF VIOLENCE & DEATH. BE CAUTIOUS!

11:24 PM · Jul 22, 2018

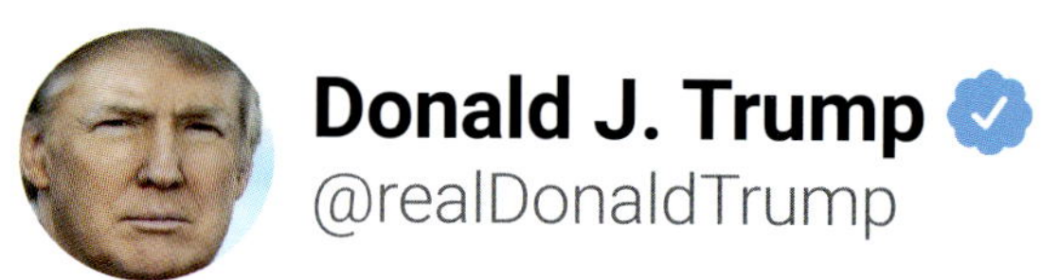

Tariffs are the greatest! Either a country which has treated the United States unfairly on Trade negotiates a fair deal, or it gets hit with Tariffs. It's as simple as that - and everybody's talking! Remember, we are the "piggy bank" that's being robbed.
All will be Great!

7:29 AM • Jul 24, 2018

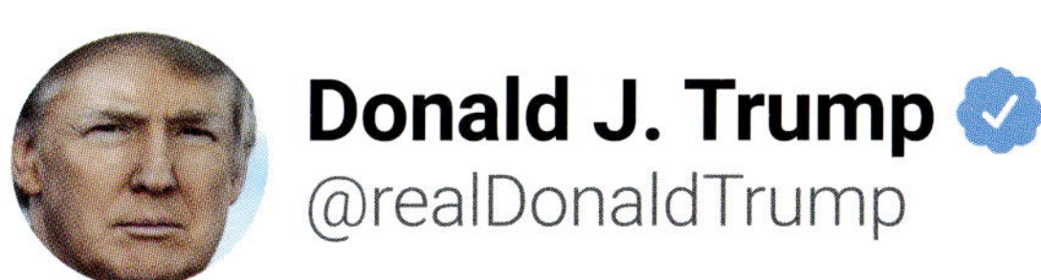

Donald J. Trump ✔
@realDonaldTrump

Please understand, there are consequences when people cross our Border illegally, whether they have children or not - and many are just using children for their own sinister purposes. Congress must act on fixing the DUMBEST & WORST immigration laws anywhere in the world! Vote "R"

7:58 AM • Jul 29, 2018

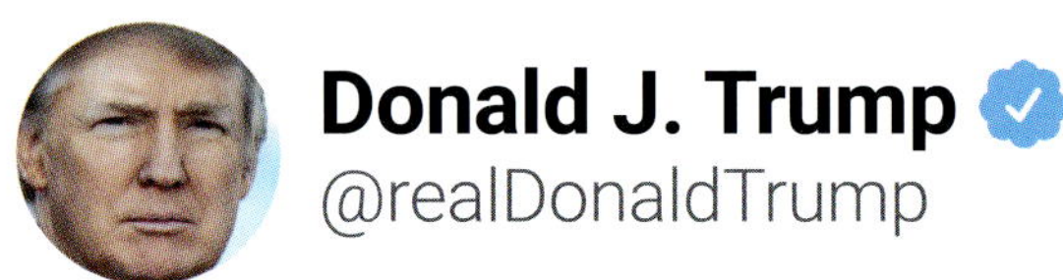

The Fake News Media is going CRAZY! They are totally unhinged and in many ways, after witnessing first hand the damage they do to so many innocent and decent people, I enjoy watching. In 7 years, when I am no longer in office, their ratings will dry up and they will be gone!

9:34 AM • Jul 31, 2018

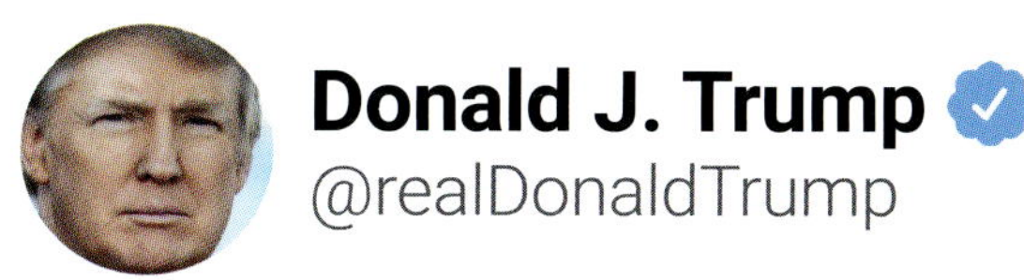

Donald J. Trump ✔
@realDonaldTrump

Lebron James was just interviewed by the dumbest man on television, Don Lemon. He made Lebron look smart, which isn't easy to do. I like Mike!

11:37 PM · Aug 3, 2018

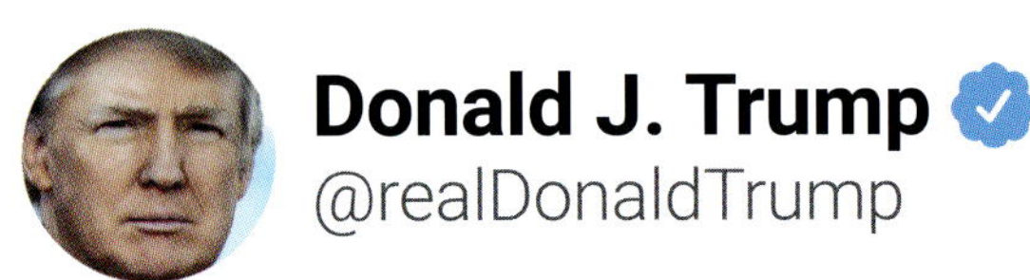

Thank you to Kanye West and the fact that he is willing to tell the TRUTH. One new and great FACT - African American unemployment is the lowest ever recorded in the history of our Country. So honored by this. Thank you Kanye for your support. It is making a big difference!

6:58 PM · Aug 10, 2018

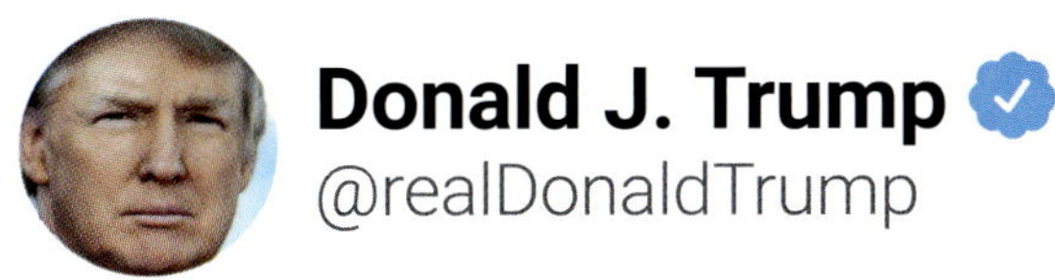

Donald J. Trump
@realDonaldTrump
If anyone is looking for a good lawyer, I would strongly suggest that you don't retain the services of Michael Cohen!
8:44 AM • Aug 22, 2018

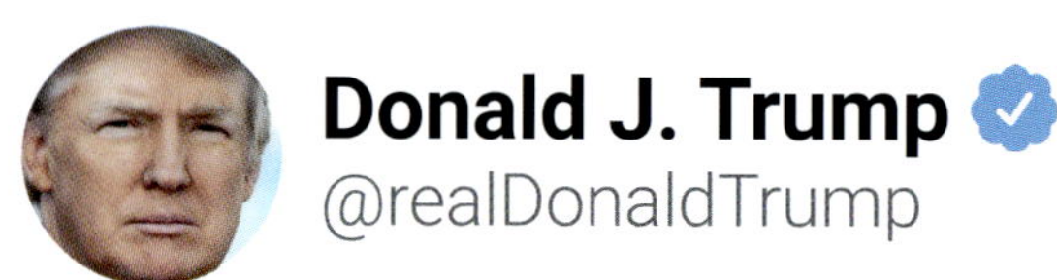

Donald J. Trump @realDonaldTrump

Over 90% approval rating for your all time favorite (I hope) President within the Republican Party and 52% overall. This despite all of the made up stories by the Fake News Media trying endlessly to make me look as bad and evil as possible. Look at the real villains please!

8:39 PM · Aug 26, 2018

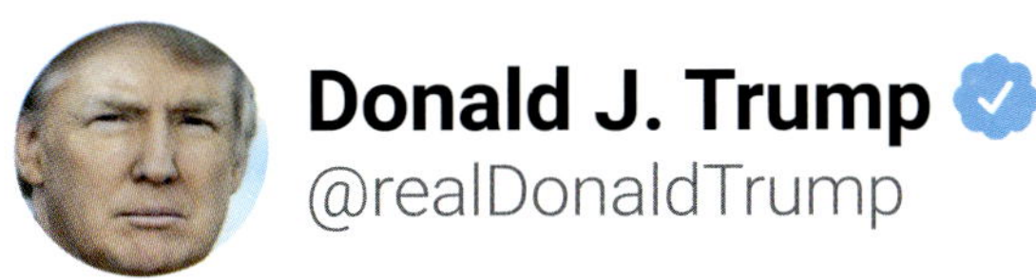

Donald J. Trump ✔
@realDonaldTrump

I'm draining the Swamp, and the Swamp is trying to fight back. Don't worry, we will win!

11:22 PM · Sep 5, 2018

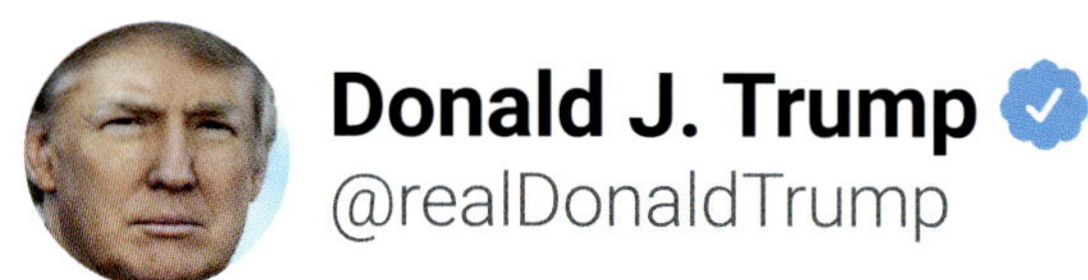

"President Trump would need a magic wand to get to 4% GDP," stated President Obama. I guess I have a magic wand, 4.2%, and we will do MUCH better than this! We have just begun.

10:42 AM • Sep 10, 2018

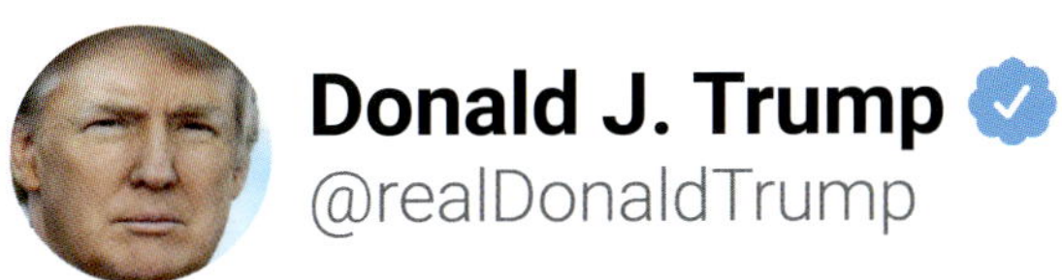

You don't hand matches to an arsonist, and you don't give power to an angry left-wing mob. Democrats have become too EXTREME and TOO DANGEROUS to govern. Republicans believe in the rule of law - not the rule of the mob. VOTE REPUBLICAN!

9:21 PM · Oct 6, 2018

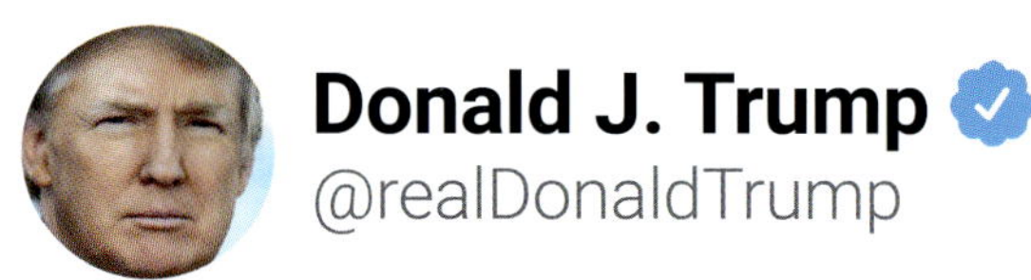

Donald J. Trump
@realDonaldTrump
Best line in the Elizabeth Warren beer catastrophe is, to her husband, "Thank you for being here. I'm glad you're here" It's their house, he's supposed to be there!
10:03 PM · Jan 13, 2019

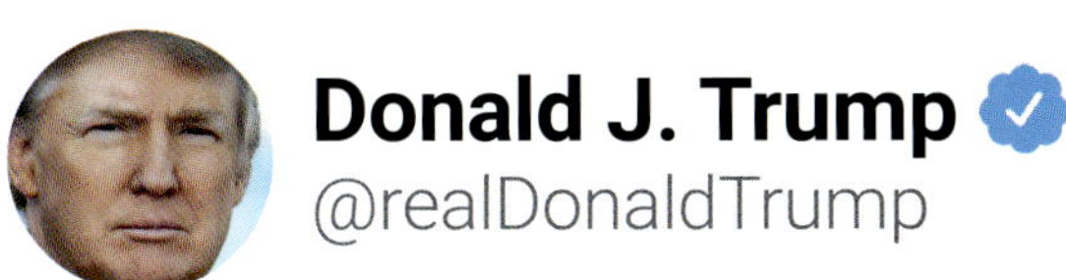

Donald J. Trump ✔
@realDonaldTrump

For decades, politicians promised to secure the border, fix
our trade deals, bring back our factories, get tough on China,
move the Embassy to Jerusalem, make NATO pay their fair
share, and so much else - only to do NOTHING (or worse)
I am doing exactly what I pledged to do, and what I was
elected to do by the citizens of our great Country. Just as
I promised, I am fighting for YOU!

5:19 PM · Jan 14, 2019

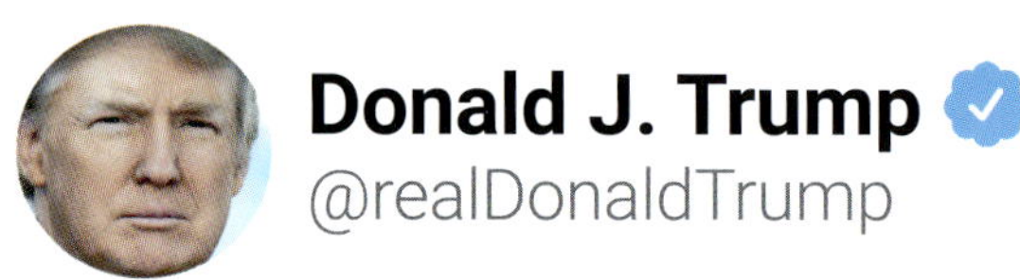

Donald J. Trump
@realDonaldTrump
Why is Nancy Pelosi getting paid when people who are working are not?
8:25 AM • Jan 15, 2019

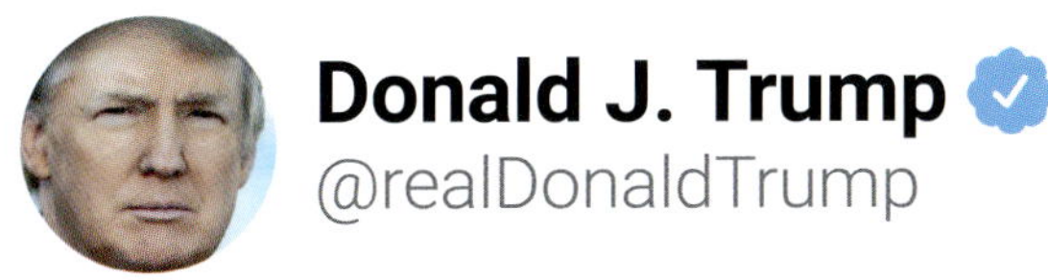

Without a Wall there cannot be safety and security at the Border or for the U.S.A. BUILD THE WALL AND CRIME WILL FALL!

8:37 AM · Jan 24, 2019

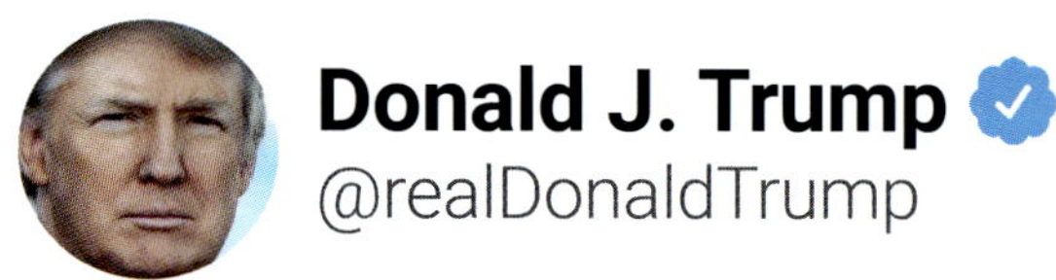

Democrats are becoming the Party of late term abortion, high taxes, Open Borders and Crime!

8:36 AM • Jan 31, 2019

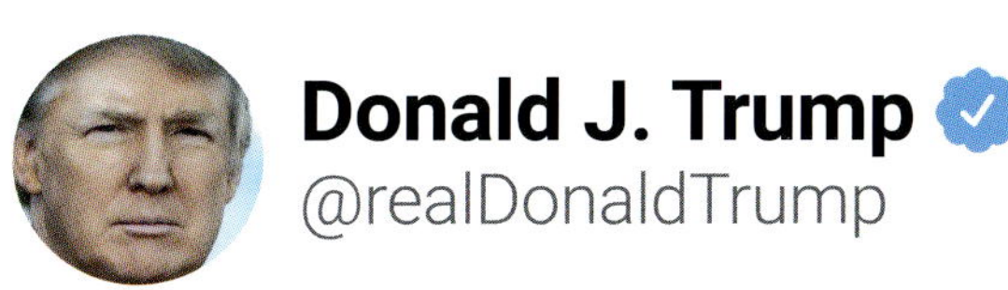

I think it is very important for the Democrats to press forward with their Green New Deal. It would be great for the so-called "Carbon Footprint" to permanently eliminate all Planes, Cars, Cows, Oil, Gas & the Military - even if no other country would do the same. Brilliant!

6:21 PM · Feb 9, 2019

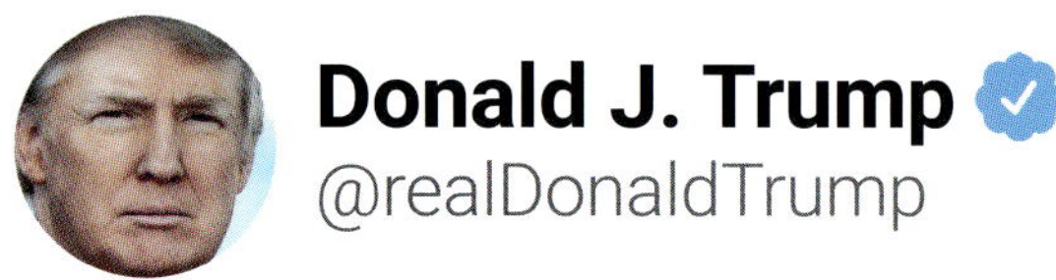

Donald J. Trump
@realDonaldTrump
THE RIGGED AND CORRUPT MEDIA IS THE ENEMY OF THE PEOPLE!
7:56 AM · Feb 17, 2019

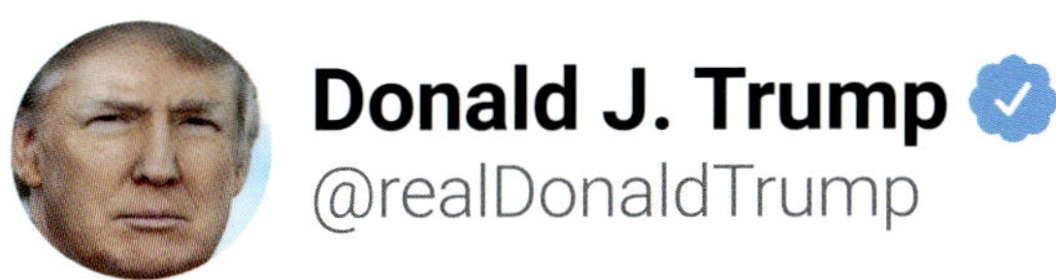

No Collusion, No Obstruction, Complete and Total EXONERATION. KEEP AMERICA GREAT!

4:42 PM • Mar 24, 2019

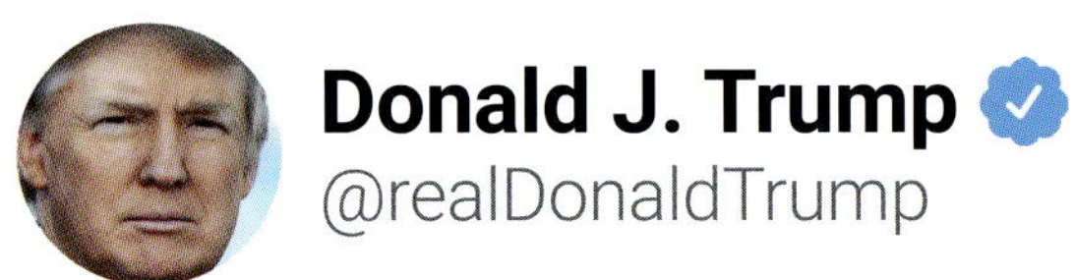

Donald J. Trump ✓
@realDonaldTrump

It would be so easy to fix our weak and very stupid Democrat inspired immigration laws. In less than one hour, and then a vote, the problem would be solved. But the Dems don't care about the crime, they don't want any victory for Trump and the Republicans, even if good for USA!

4:31 PM · Mar 30, 2019

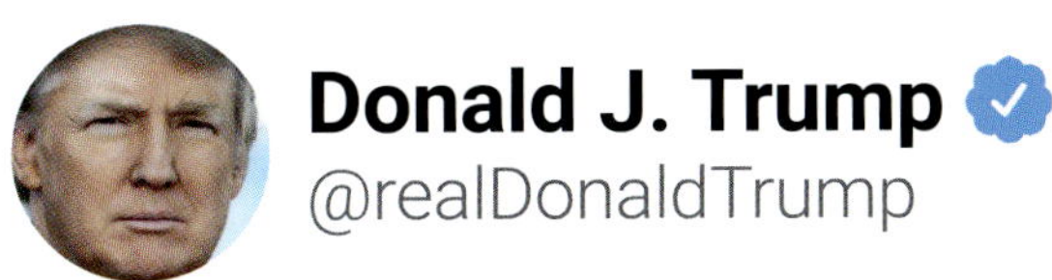

Donald J. Trump ✔
@realDonaldTrump

There is nothing we can ever give to the Democrats that will make them happy. This is the highest level of Presidential Harassment in the history of our Country!

8:46 AM • Apr 4, 2019

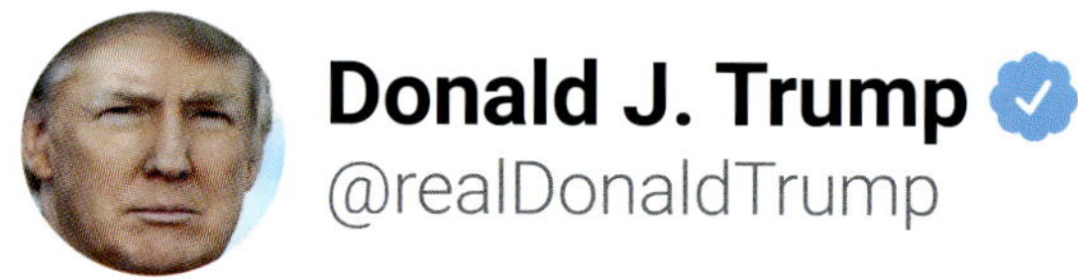

Donald J. Trump
@realDonaldTrump
THEY SPIED ON MY CAMPAIGN (We will never forget)!
9:52 AM · Apr 15, 2019

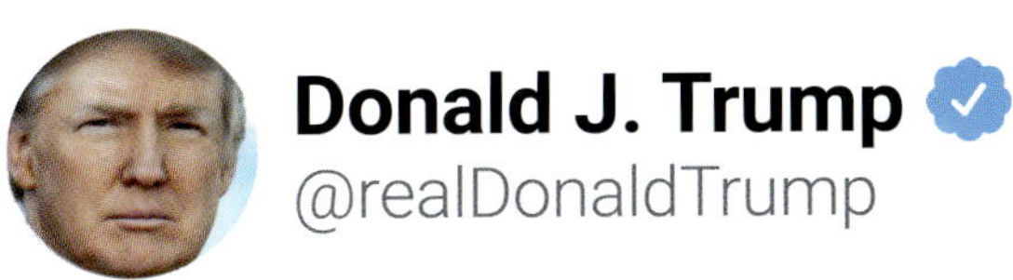

How do you impeach a Republican President for a crime that was committed by the Democrats? MAKE AMERICA GREAT AGAIN!

6:35 PM · Apr 21, 2019

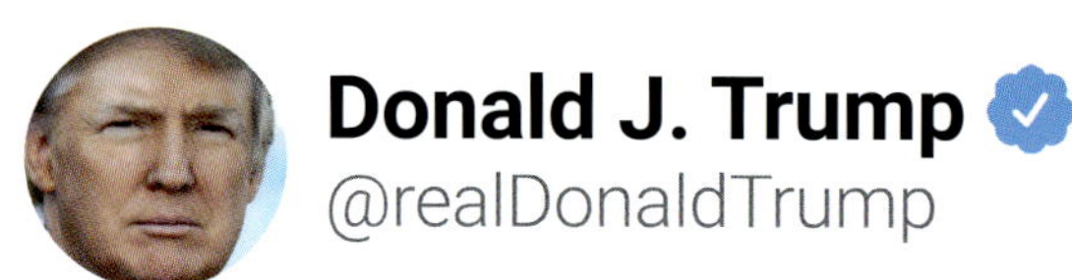

Donald J. Trump ✔
@realDonaldTrump

"President Donald J. Trump is the greatest hostage negotiator that I know of in the history of the United States. 20 hostages, many in impossible circumstances, have been released in last two years. No money was paid." Cheif Hostage Negotiator, USA!

7:32 AM • Apr 26, 2019

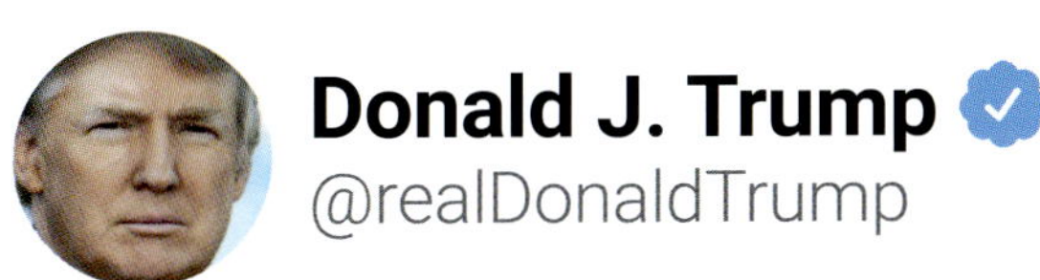 **Donald J. Trump** ✔
@realDonaldTrump

On this day of prayer, we once again place our hopes in the hands of our Creator. We give thanks for this wondrous land of liberty, & we pray that THIS nation – OUR home – these United States – will forever be strengthened by the Goodness and the Grace & the eternal GLORY OF GOD!

4:55 PM • May 2, 2019

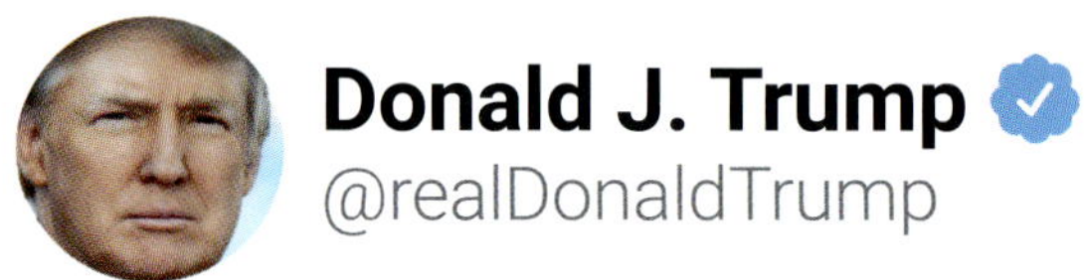

I am continuing to monitor the censorship of AMERICAN CITIZENS on social media platforms. This is the United States of America — and we have what's known as FREEDOM OF SPEECH! We are monitoring and watching, closely!!

6:55 PM • May 3, 2019

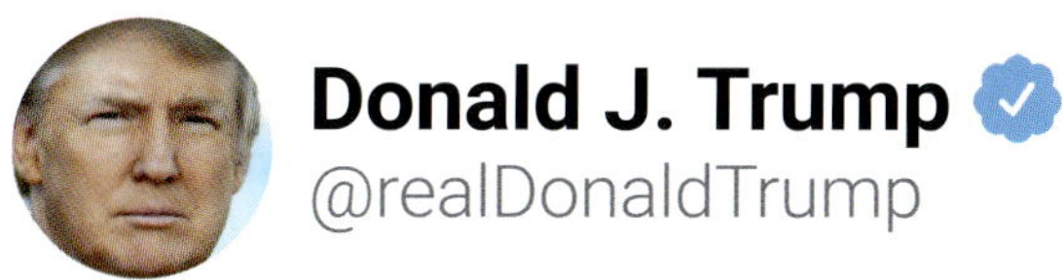

Donald J. Trump
@realDonaldTrump
Such an easy way to avoid Tariffs? Make or produce your goods and products in the good old USA. It's very simple!
9:55 AM · May 11, 2019

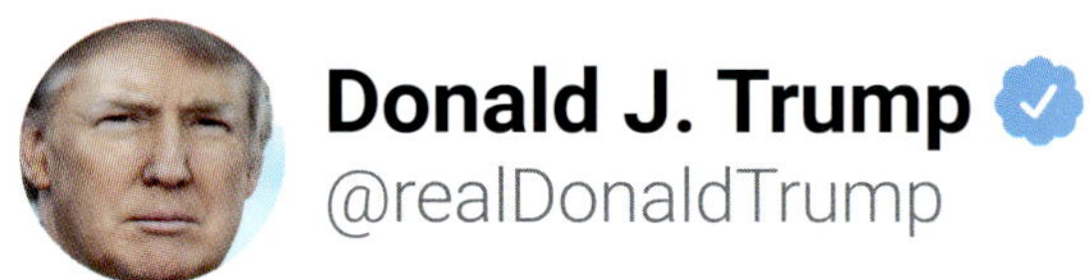

Donald J. Trump ✔
@realDonaldTrump

My Campaign for President was conclusively spied on.
Nothing like this has ever happened in American Politics.
A really bad situation. TREASON means long jail sentences,
and this was TREASON!

7:11 AM • May 17, 2019

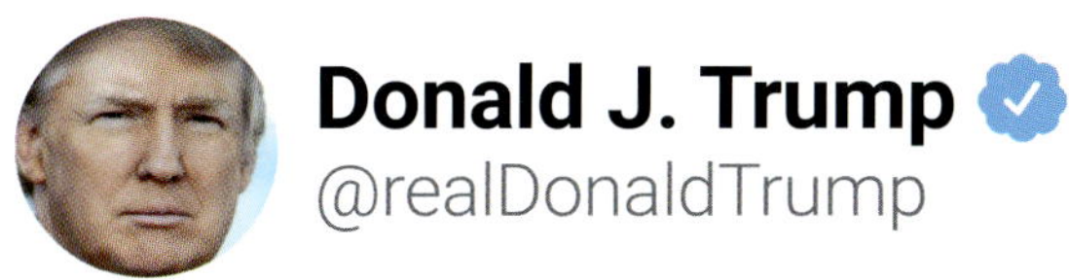

Donald J. Trump ✓
@realDonaldTrump

If Iran wants to fight, that will be the official end of Iran.
Never threaten the United States again!

4:25 PM • May 19, 2019

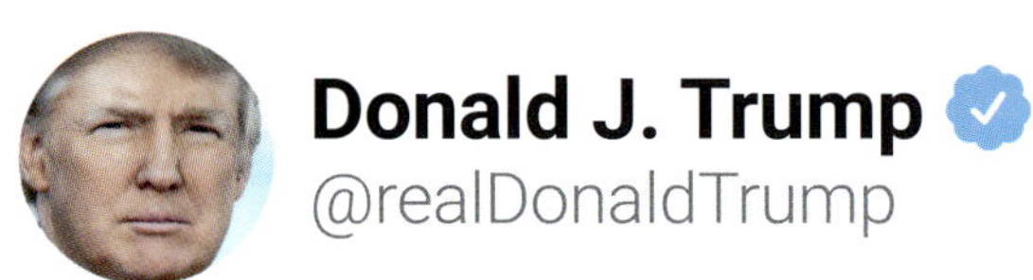

I was actually sticking up for Sleepy Joe Biden while on foreign soil. Kim Jong Un called him a "low IQ idiot," and many other things, whereas I related the quote of Chairman Kim as a much softer "low IQ individual." Who could possibly be upset with that?

5:58 PM · May 28, 2019

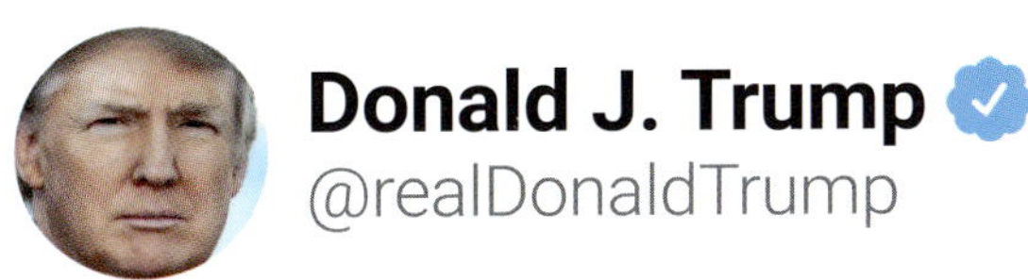

Twitter should let the banned Conservative Voices back onto their platform, without restriction. It's called Freedom of Speech, remember. You are making a Giant Mistake!

8:45 AM · Jun 9, 2019

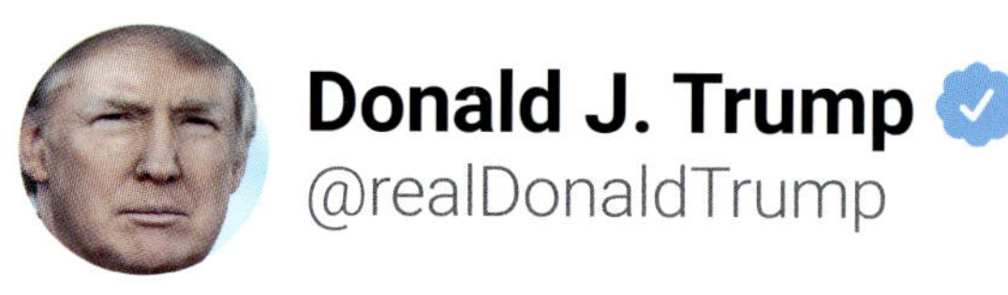

94% Approval Rating in the Republican Party, an all time high. Ronald Reagan was 87%. Thank you!

5:21 PM · Jul 13, 2019

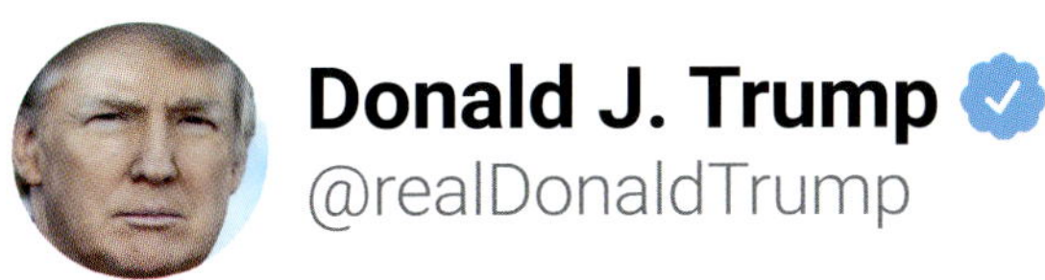

Donald J. Trump ✔
@realDonaldTrump

We will never be a Socialist or Communist Country. IF YOU ARE NOT HAPPY HERE, YOU CAN LEAVE! It is your choice, and your choice alone. This is about love for America. Certain people HATE our Country. They are anti-Israel, pro Al-Qaeda, and comment on the 9/11 attack, "some people did something." Radical Left Democrats want Open Borders, which means drugs, crime, human trafficking, and much more. Detention facilities are not Concentration Camps! America has never been stronger than it is now – rebuilt Military, highest Stock Market EVER, lowest unemployment and more people working than ever before. Keep America Great!

5:08 PM ▪ Jul 15, 2019

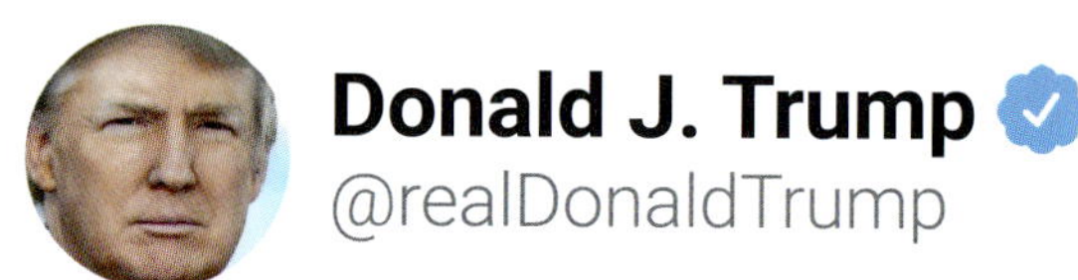

Donald J. Trump ✓
@realDonaldTrump

The Obama Administration built the Cages, not the Trump Administration! DEMOCRATS MUST GIVE US THE VOTES TO CHANGE BAD IMMIGRATION LAWS.

5:43 PM · Jul 15, 2019

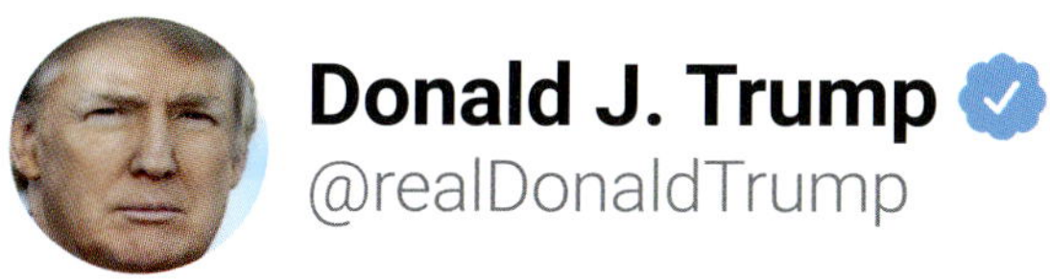

Our Country is Free, Beautiful and Very Successful. If you hate our Country, or if you are not happy here, you can leave!

8:17 AM · Jul 16, 2019

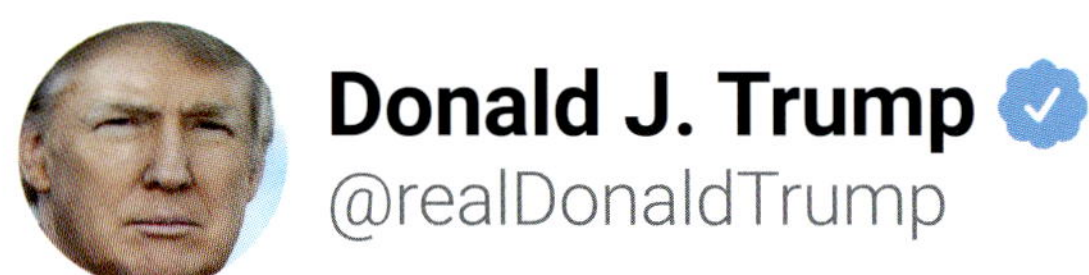

Those Tweets were NOT Racist. I don't have a Racist bone in my body! The so-called vote to be taken is a Democrat con game. Republicans should not show "weakness" and fall into their trap. This should be a vote on the filthy language, statements and lies told by the Democrat Congresswomen, who I truly believe, based on their actions, hate our Country. Get a list of the HORRIBLE things they have said. Omar is polling at 8%, Cortez at 21%. Nancy Pelosi tried to push them away, but now they are forever wedded to the Democrat Party. See you in 2020!

9:59 AM · Jul 16, 2019

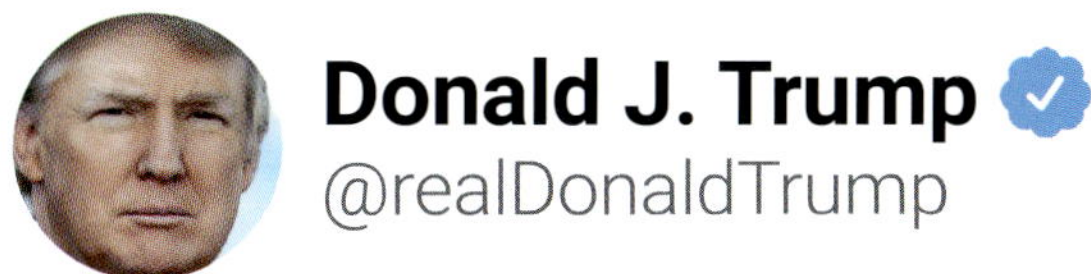

Donald J. Trump ✔
@realDonaldTrump

TRUTH IS A FORCE OF NATURE!

3:33 PM · Jul 24, 2019

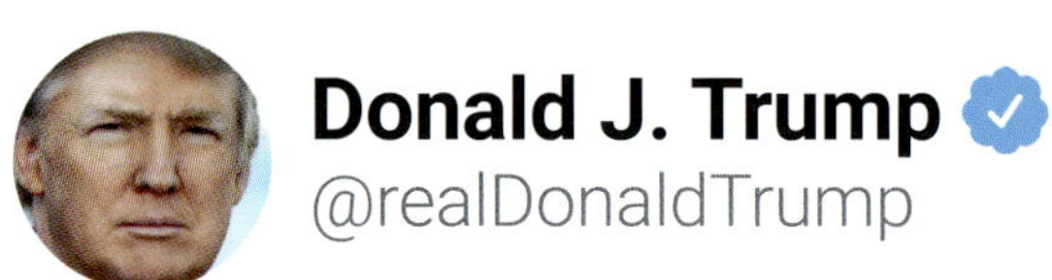

Donald J. Trump ✔
@realDonaldTrump

Never has the press been more inaccurate, unfair or corrupt!
We are not fighting the Democrats, they are easy, we are
fighting the seriously dishonest and unhinged Lamestream
Media. They have gone totally CRAZY. MAKE AMERICA
GREAT AGAIN!

8:07 AM • Aug 10, 2019

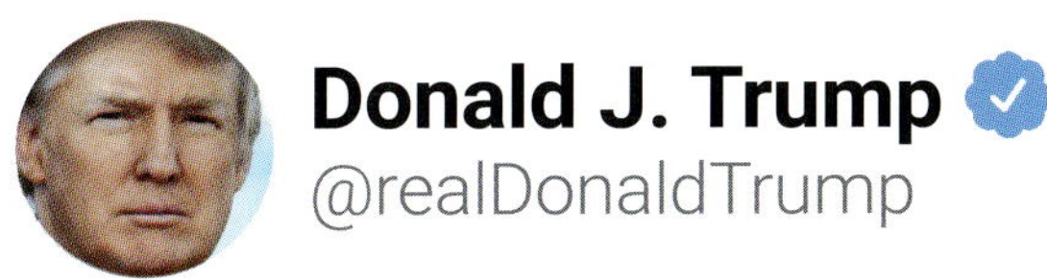

I donate 100% of my President's salary, $400,000, back to our Country, and feel very good about it!

6:52 PM · Aug 16, 2019

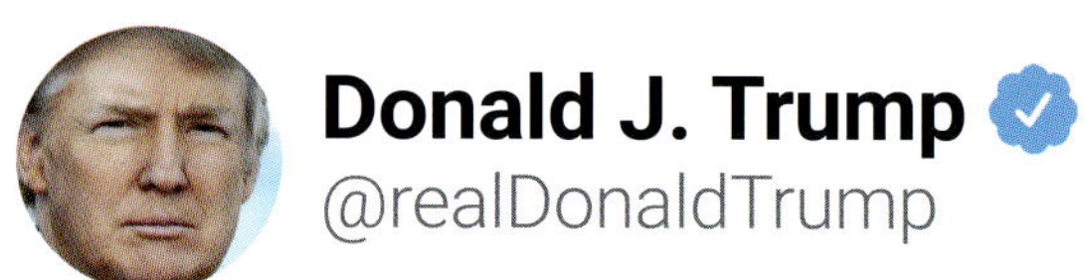

Wow, Report Just Out! Google manipulated from 2.6 million to 16 million votes for Hillary Clinton in 2016 Election! This was put out by a Clinton supporter, not a Trump Supporter! Google should be sued. My victory was even bigger than thought! @JudicialWatch

11:52 AM · Aug 19, 2019

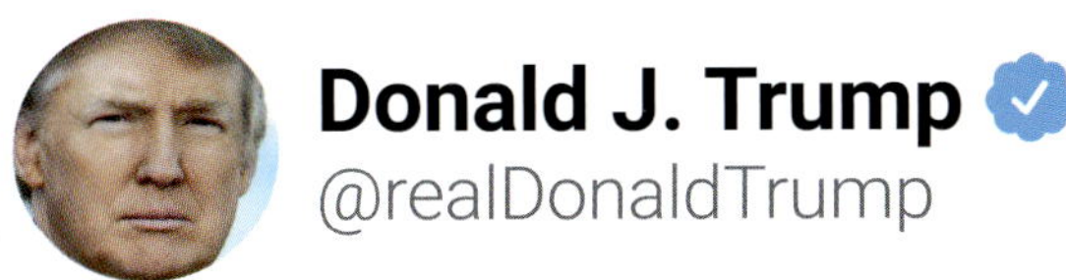

Donald J. Trump ✓
@realDonaldTrump

PRESIDENTIAL HARASSMENT!

5:17 PM · Sep 24, 2019

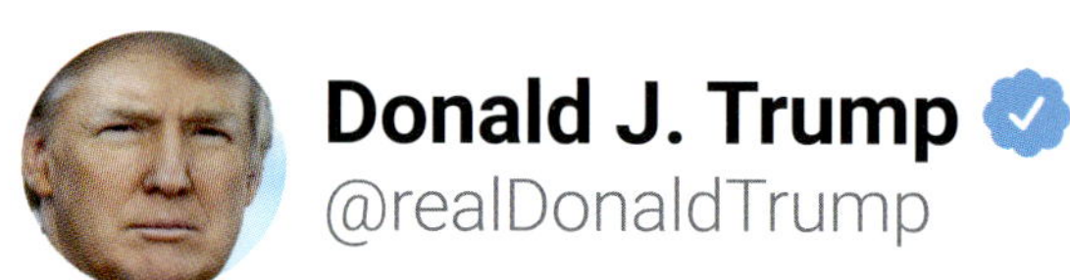

There has been no President in the history of our Country who has been treated so badly as I have. The Democrats are frozen with hatred and fear. They get nothing done. This should never be allowed to happen to another President. Witch Hunt!

7:24 AM • Sep 25, 2019

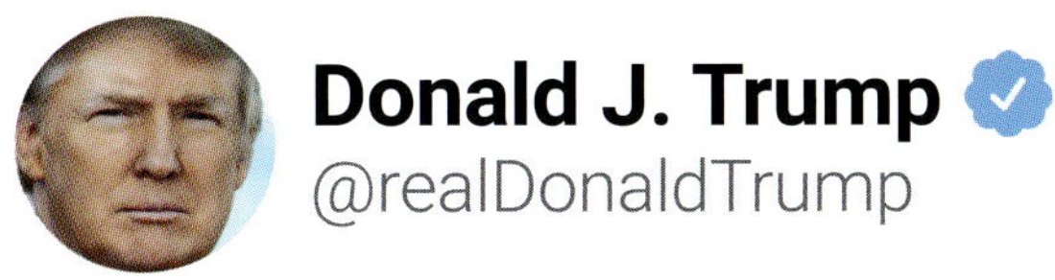

Donald J. Trump ✔
@realDonaldTrump

They are trying to stop ME, because I am fighting for YOU!

5:14 PM · Sep 28, 2019

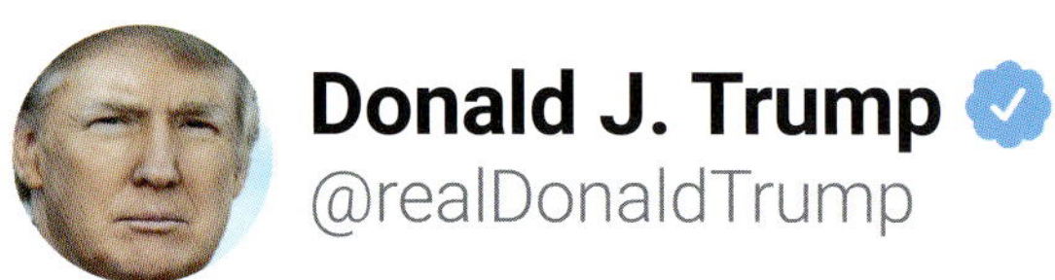

As I learn more and more each day, I am coming to the conclusion that what is taking place is not an impeachment, it is a COUP, intended to take away the Power of the People, their VOTE, their Freedoms, their Second Amendment, Religion, Military, Border Wall, and their God-given rights as a Citizen of The United States of America!

7:41 PM · Oct 1, 2019

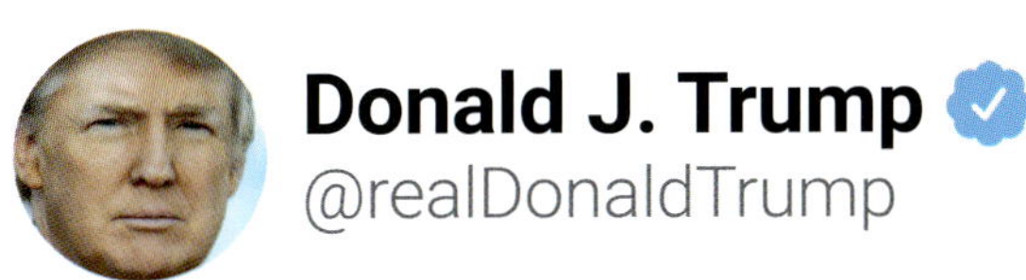

The Do Nothing Democrats should be focused on building up our Country, not wasting everyone's time and energy on BULLSHIT, which is what they have been doing ever since I got overwhelmingly elected in 2016, 223-306. Get a better candidate this time, you'll need it!

11:48 AM · Oct 2, 2019

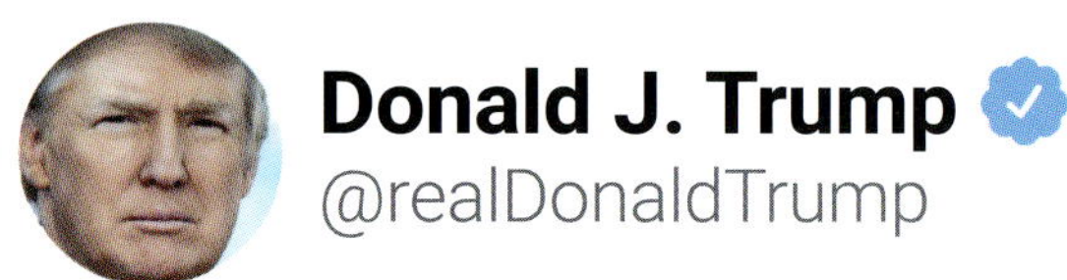

Donald J. Trump
@realDonaldTrump

So Crooked Hillary Clinton can delete and acid wash 33,000 emails AFTER getting a Subpoena from the United States Congress, but I can't make one totally appropriate telephone call to the President of Ukraine? Witch Hunt!

3:25 PM · Oct 5, 2019

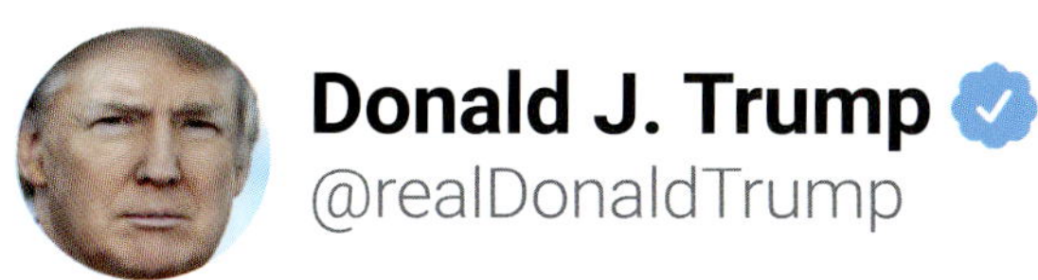

Donald J. Trump ✓
@realDonaldTrump

I was elected on getting out of these ridiculous endless wars, where our great Military functions as a policing operation to the benefit of people who don't even like the USA. The two most unhappy countries at this move are Russia & China, because they love seeing us bogged down, watching over a quagmire, & spending big dollars to do so. When I took over, our Military was totally depleted. Now it is stronger than ever before. The endless and ridiculous wars are ENDING! We will be focused on the big picture, knowing we can always go back & BLAST!

11:20 AM • Oct 7, 2019

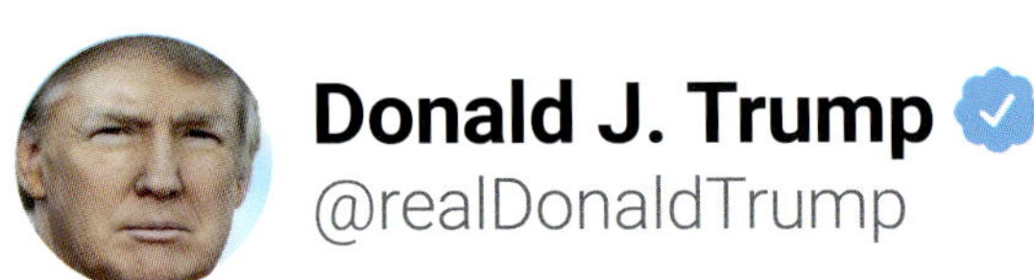

As I have stated strongly before, and just to reiterate, if Turkey does anything that I, in my great and unmatched wisdom, consider to be off limits, I will totally destroy and obliterate the Economy of Turkey (I've done before!). They must, with Europe and others, watch over the captured ISIS fighters and families. The U.S. has done far more than anyone could have ever expected, including the capture of 100% of the ISIS Caliphate. It is time now for others in the region, some of great wealth, to protect their own territory. THE USA IS GREAT!

11:38 AM • Oct 7, 2019

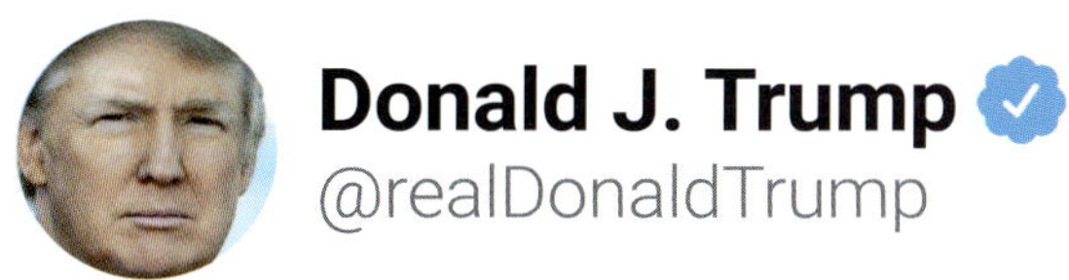

Donald J. Trump
@realDonaldTrump
You can't Impeach someone who hasn't done anything wrong!
6:48 PM · Nov 1, 2019

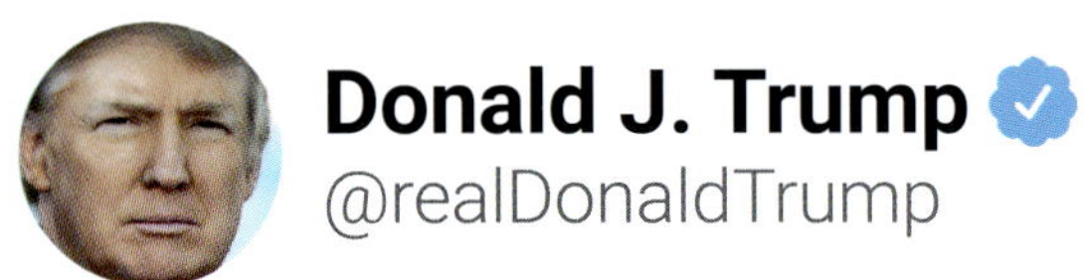

Donald J. Trump ✔
@realDonaldTrump

So ridiculous. Greta must work on her Anger Management problem, then go to a good old fashioned movie with a friend! Chill Greta, Chill!

7:22 AM · Dec 12, 2019

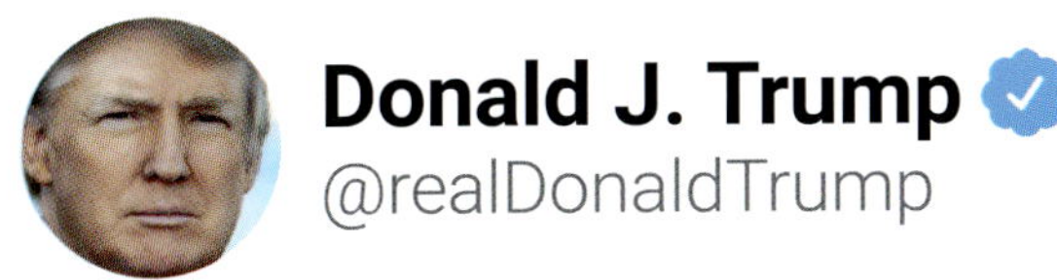

Donald J. Trump
@realDonaldTrump
I JUST GOT IMPEACHED FOR MAKING A PERFECT PHONE CALL!
3:39 PM · Jan 16, 2020

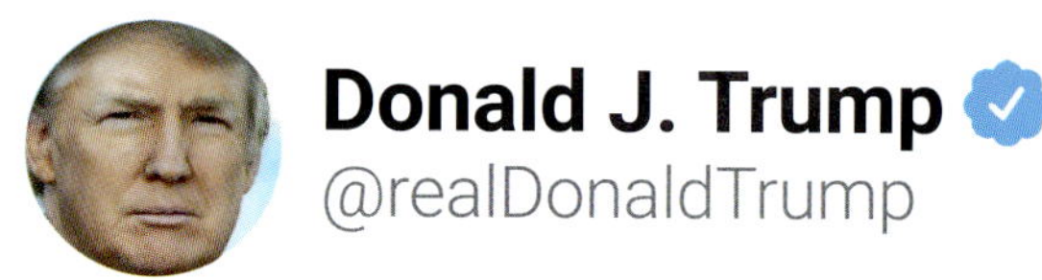

Peaceful protests are a hallmark of our democracy. Even if I don't always agree, I recognize the rights of people to express their views.

9:23 AM · Jan 22, 2020

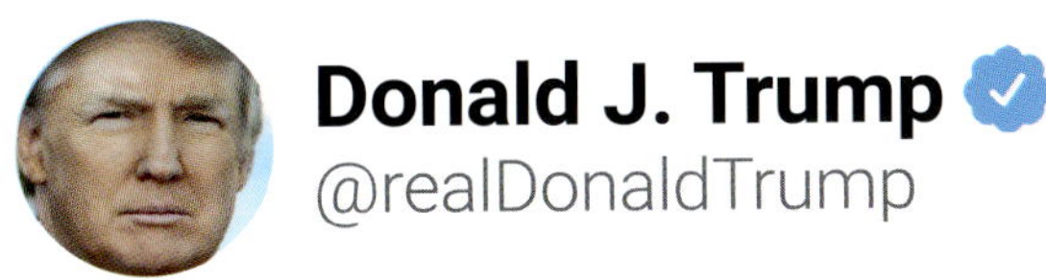

Donald J. Trump
@realDonaldTrump
The world is at war with a hidden enemy. WE WILL WIN!
3:31 PM · Mar 17, 2020

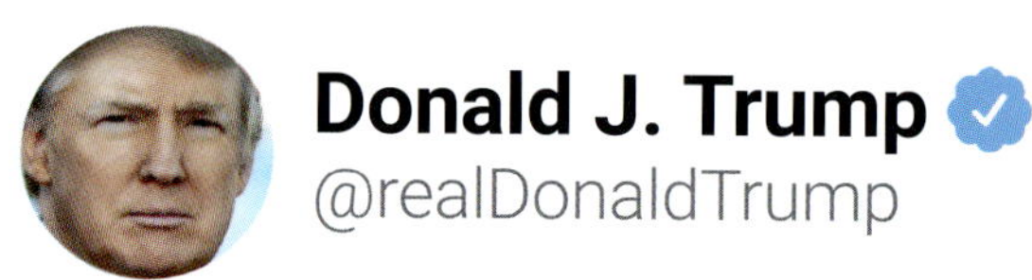

Donald J. Trump @realDonaldTrump

I always treated the Chinese Virus very seriously, and have done a very good job from the beginning, including my very early decision to close the "borders" from China - against the wishes of almost all. Many lives were saved. The Fake News new narrative is disgraceful & false!

7:46 AM • Mar 18, 2020

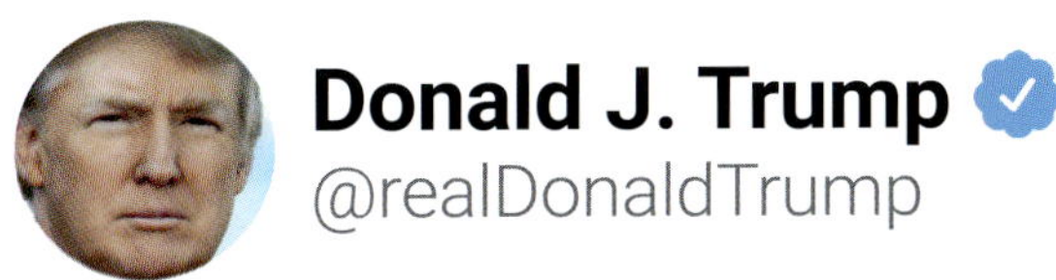

Remember, the Cure can't be worse than the problem itself. Be careful, be safe, use common sense!

6:17 PM · Apr 25, 2020

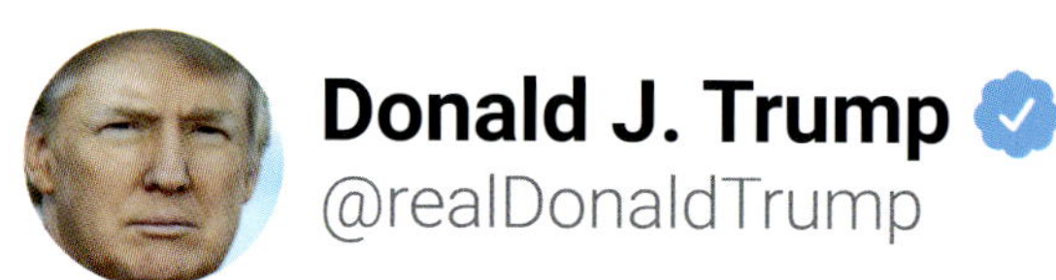

Donald J. Trump ✓
@realDonaldTrump

I never said the pandemic was a Hoax! Who would say such a thing? I said that the Do Nothing Democrats, together with their Mainstream Media partners, are the Hoax. They have been called out & embarrassed on this, even admitting they were wrong, but continue to spread the lie!

6:23 PM · Apr 25, 2020

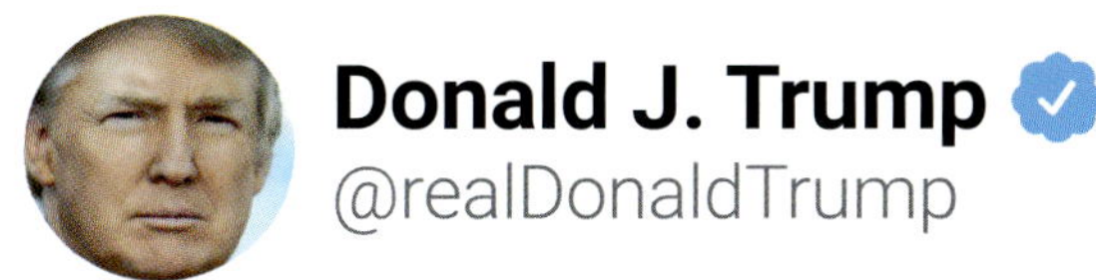

Donald J. Trump
@realDonaldTrump
OBAMAGATE makes Watergate look small time!
10:16 AM · May 11, 2020

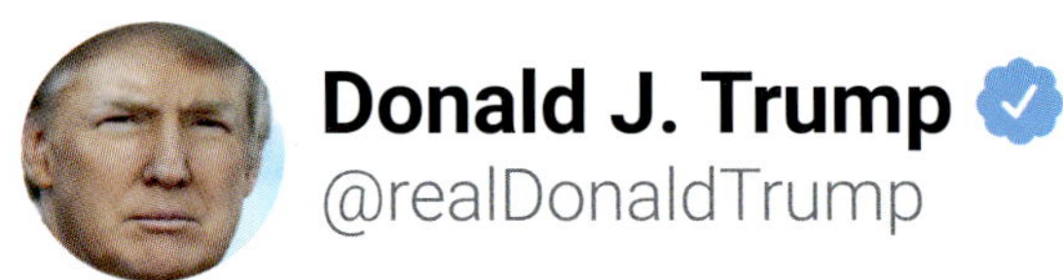

Donald J. Trump
@realDonaldTrump

Thank you to all of my great Keyboard Warriors. You are better, and far more brilliant, than anyone on Madison Avenue (Ad Agencies). There is nobody like you!

10:47 PM • May 14, 2020

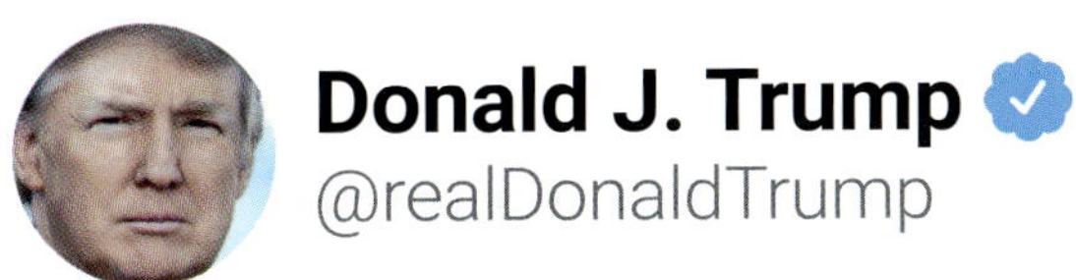

Donald J. Trump ✓
@realDonaldTrump

The Obama Administration is turning out to be one of the most corrupt and incompetent in U.S. history. Remember, he and Sleepy Joe are the reasons I am in the White House!!!

3:28 PM · May 17, 2020

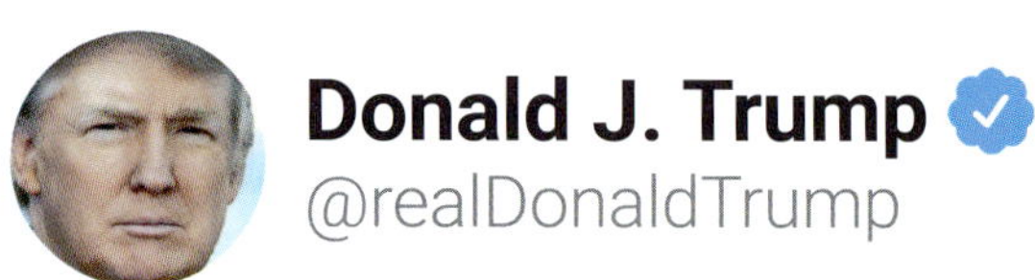

@Twitter is now interfering in the 2020 Presidential Election. They are saying my statement on Mail-In Ballots, which will lead to massive corruption and fraud, is incorrect, based on fact-checking by Fake News CNN and the Amazon Washington Post. Twitter is completely stifling FREE SPEECH, and I, as President, will not allow it to happen!

7:40 PM • May 26, 2020

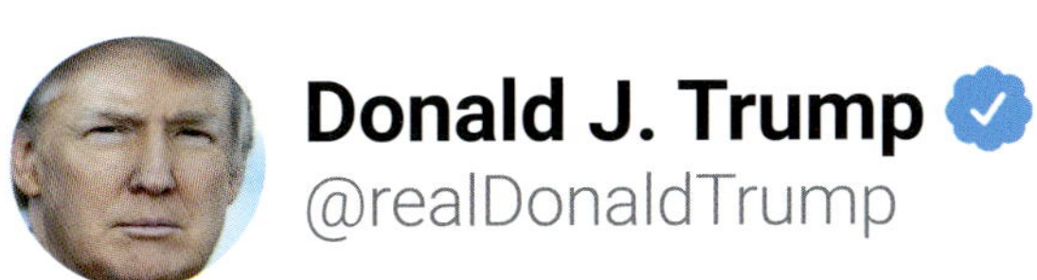

Donald J. Trump ✔
@realDonaldTrump

Sleepy Joe has been in politics for 40 years, and did nothing. Now he pretends to have the answers. He doesn't even know the questions. Weakness will never beat anarchists, looters or thugs, and Joe has been politically weak all of his life. LAW & ORDER!

3:56 PM · Jun 2, 2020

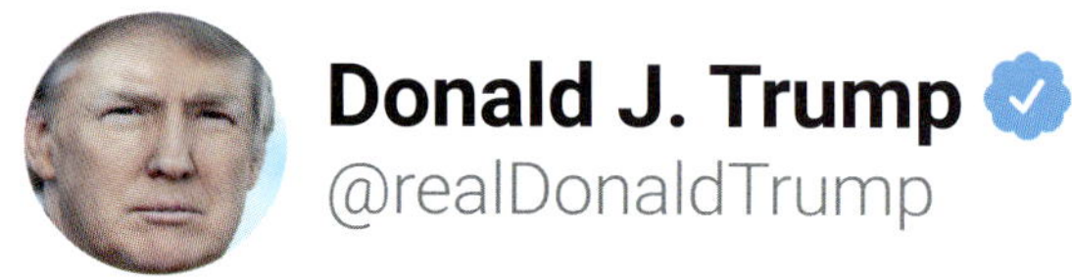

Donald J. Trump
@realDonaldTrump

YOU DON'T BURN CHURCHES IN AMERICA!

6:28 PM · Jun 4, 2020

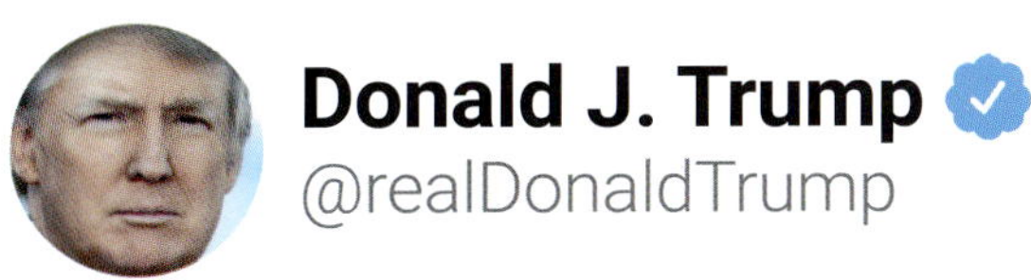

Sleepy Joe Biden and the Radical Left Democrats want to "DEFUND THE POLICE". I want great and well paid LAW ENFORCEMENT. I want LAW & ORDER!

9:09 AM • Jun 7, 2020

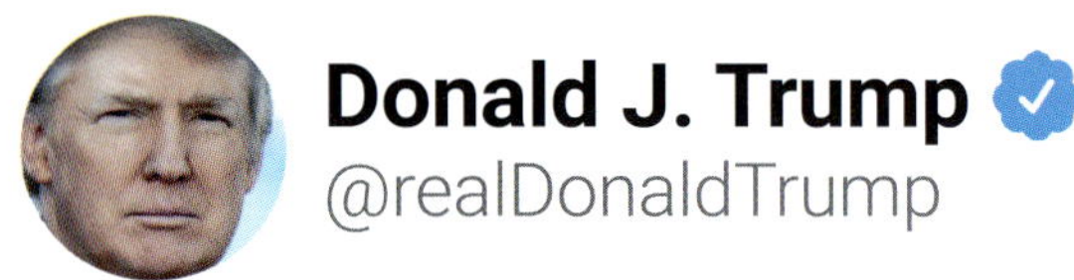

THOSE THAT DENY THEIR HISTORY ARE DOOMED TO REPEAT IT!

10:09 AM · Jun 11, 2020

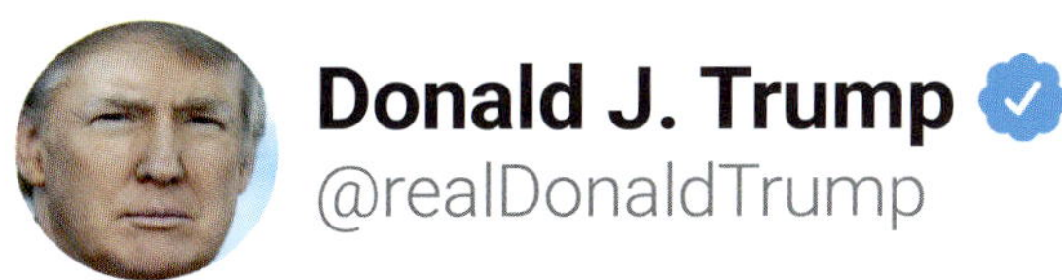

Donald J. Trump ✔
@realDonaldTrump

The Radical Left Democrats: First they try to take away your guns. Then they try to take away your police!

9:24 PM · Jun 11, 2020

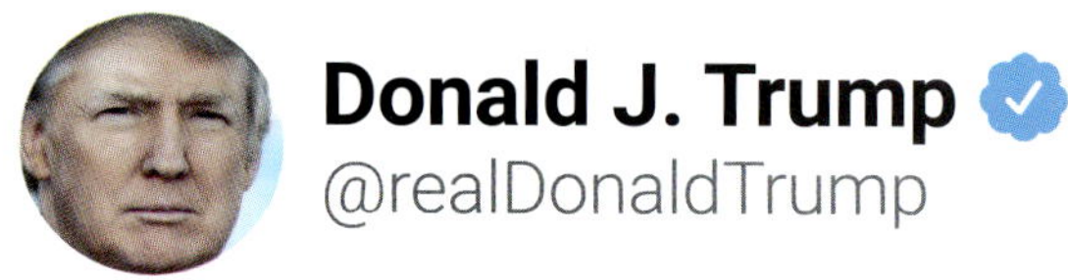

Donald J. Trump
@realDonaldTrump
THE SILENT MAJORITY IS STRONGER THAN EVER!!!
5:54 PM • Jun 14, 2020

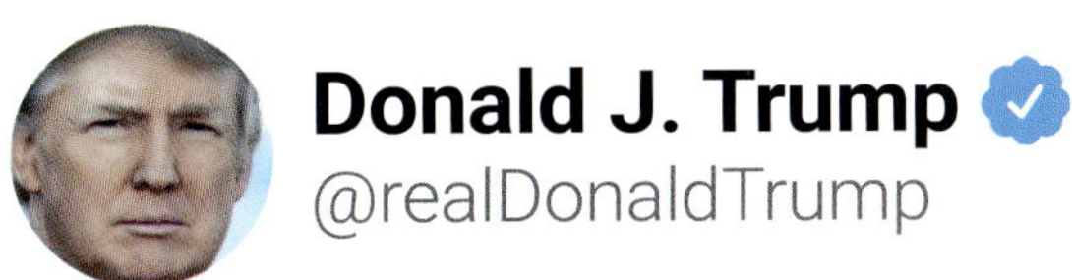

Donald J. Trump ✓
@realDonaldTrump

So we catch Obama & Biden, not to even mention the rest of their crew, SPYING on my campaign, AND NOTHING HAPPENS? I hope not! If it were the other way around, 50 years for treason. NEVER FORGET!!!!

1:14 PM · Jul 19, 2020

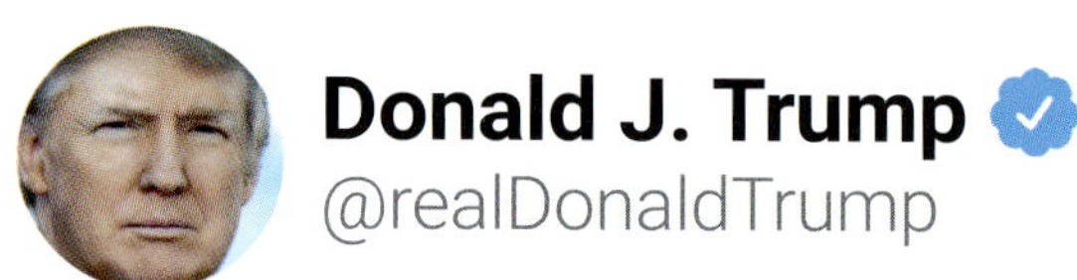

Donald J. Trump ✔
@realDonaldTrump

Big Pharma is taking television ads trying to make the case that I am raising prescription drug prices on seniors. The ad is a lie! What I have done will lead to a 50% REDUCTION in prices, at least, & Big Pharma is not happy about it. No other President would be able to produce what I have. So when you see those nasty ads from Big Pharma remember, the only reason they are going all out is the massive PRICE REDUCTIONS you are getting - not good for them. Plus, I was only President in 51 years that got a Prescription D reduction!

9:48 AM • Jul 28, 2020

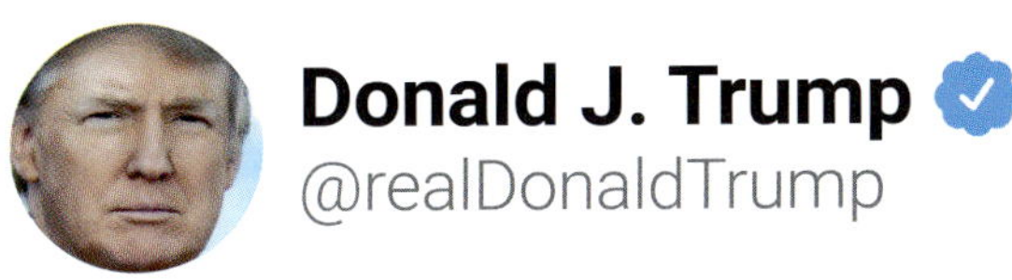

Donald J. Trump ✔
@realDonaldTrump

A$AP Rocky released from prison and on his way home to the United States from Sweden. It was a Rocky Week, get home ASAP A$AP!

1:41 PM • Aug 2, 2020

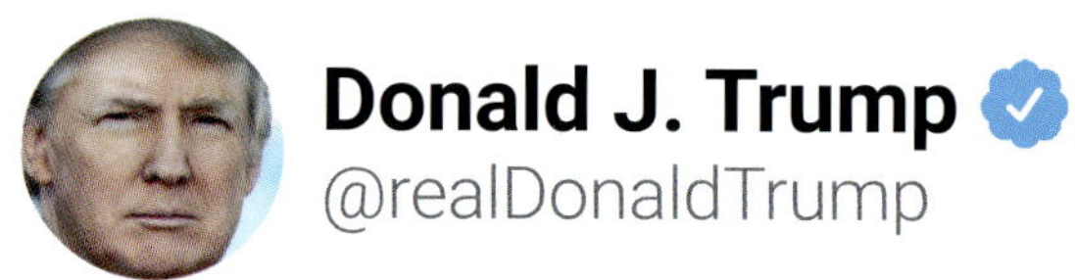

Donald J. Trump
@realDonaldTrump
FAKE NEWS IS THE ENEMY OF THE PEOPLE!
7:49 AM · Aug 3, 2020

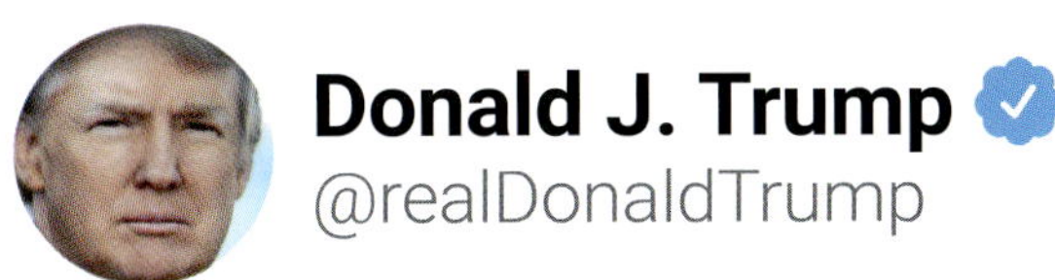

Donald J. Trump ✓
@realDonaldTrump

Somebody please explain to @MichelleObama that Donald J. Trump would not be here, in the beautiful White House, if it weren't for the job done by your husband, Barack Obama. Biden was merely an afterthought, a good reason for that very late & unenthusiastic endorsement. My Administration and I built the greatest economy in history, of any country, turned it off, saved millions of lives, and now am building an even greater economy than it was before. Jobs are flowing, NASDAQ is already at a record high, the rest to follow. Sit back & watch!

7:00 AM • Aug 18, 2020

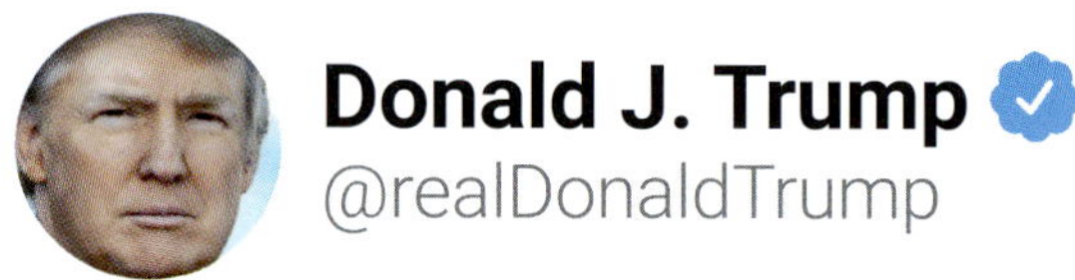

Donald J. Trump ✔
@realDonaldTrump

IF YOU CAN PROTEST IN PERSON, YOU CAN VOTE IN PERSON!

9:38 AM · Aug 19, 2020

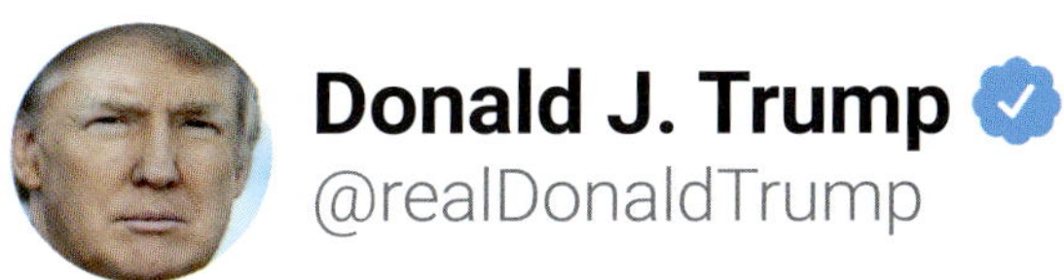

Donald J. Trump ✔
@realDonaldTrump

The Ten Most Dangerous Cities in the U.S. are ALL run by Democrats, and this has gone on for DECADES!

7:07 PM · Aug 27, 2020

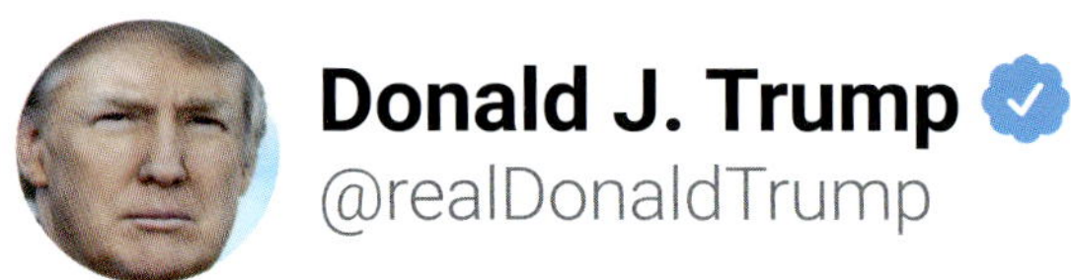

Nancy Pelosi says she got "set up" by a Beauty Parlor owner. Maybe the Beauty Parlor owner should be running the House of Representatives instead of Crazy Nancy?

2:27 PM · Sep 3, 2020

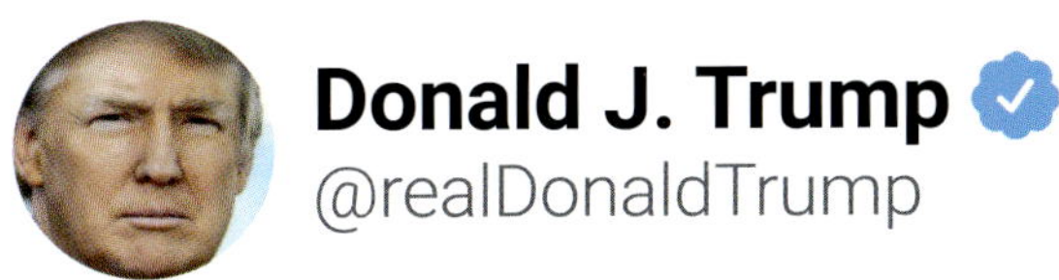

Donald J. Trump ✔
@realDonaldTrump

Joe Biden just announced that he will not agree to a
Drug Test. Gee, I wonder why?

10:33 AM • Sep 28, 2020

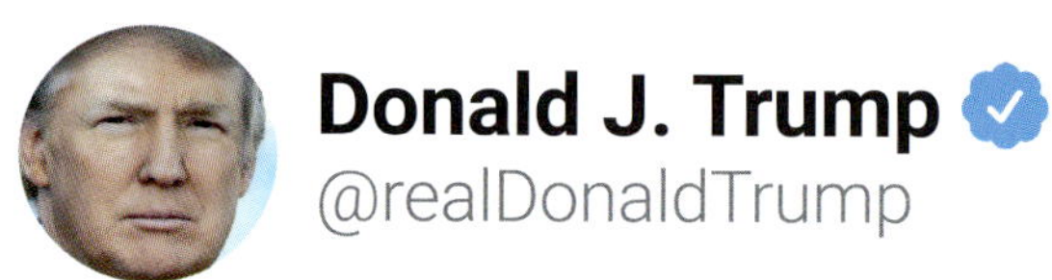

Donald J. Trump ✔
@realDonaldTrump

IF YOU WANT A MASSIVE TAX INCREASE, THE BIGGEST IN THE HISTORY OF OUR COUNTRY (AND ONE THAT WILL SHUT OUR ECONOMY AND JOBS DOWN), VOTE DEMOCRAT!!!

6:30 AM · Oct 5, 2020

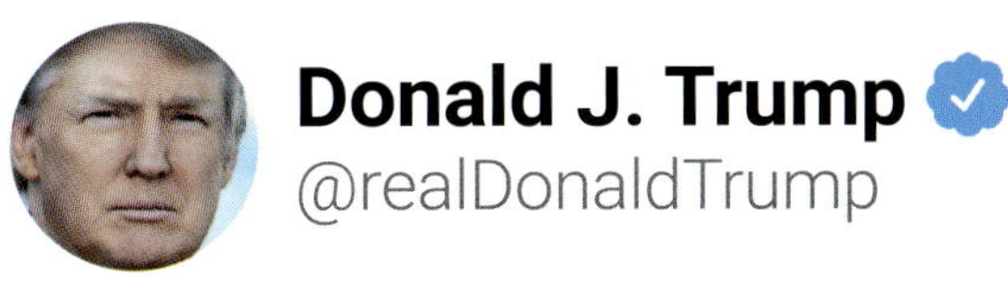

Donald J. Trump
@realDonaldTrump
GIANT RED WAVE COMING!
12:01 PM • Oct 17, 2020

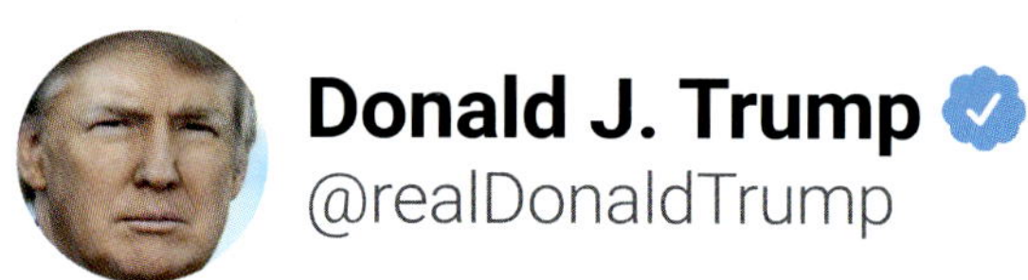

Donald J. Trump
@realDonaldTrump
Joe Biden called me George yesterday. Couldn't remember my name. Got some help from the anchor to get him through the interview. The Fake News Cartel is working overtime to cover it up!
7:30 AM • Oct 26, 2020

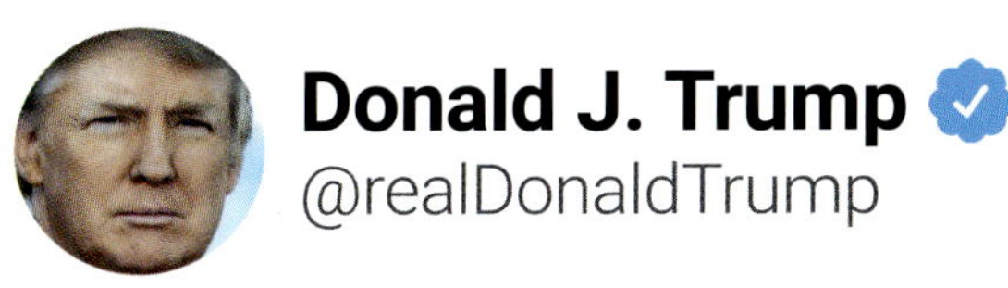

Why isn't Twitter trending Biden corruption? It's the biggest, and most credible, story anywhere in the world. Fake Trending!!!

2:54 PM · Oct 28, 2020

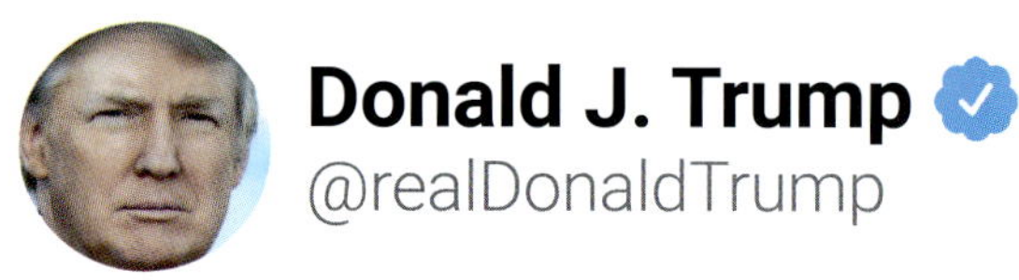

Donald J. Trump ✓
@realDonaldTrump

Biden was a pathetic laughing stock all over Washington for the horrible way he handled the H1N1 Swine Flu. Even his own Chief of Staff said he didn't know what he was doing!

1:08 PM · Nov 2, 2020

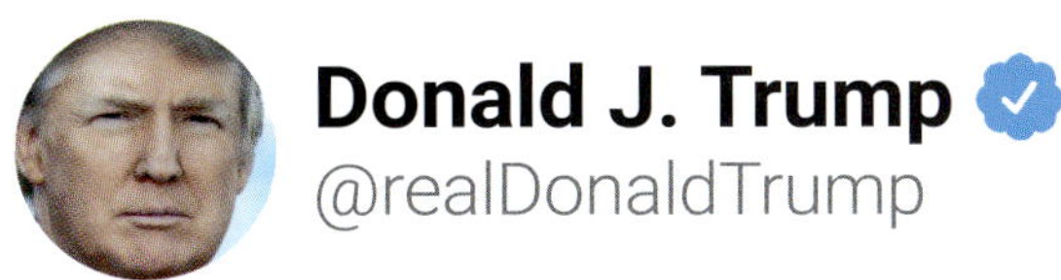

Donald J. Trump ✓
@realDonaldTrump

Joe Biden is a globalist who spent 47 years outsourcing your jobs, opening your borders, and sacrificing American blood and treasure in endless foreign wars. He shuttered your steel mills, annihilated your coal jobs, and supported every disastrous trade deal for half a century. He was a cheerleader for NAFTA and China's entry into the WTO. Pennsylvania lost half of its manufacturing jobs after those Biden Calamities. Joe Biden is a corrupt politician who SOLD OUT Pennsylvania to CHINA!

4:24 PM · Nov 2, 2020

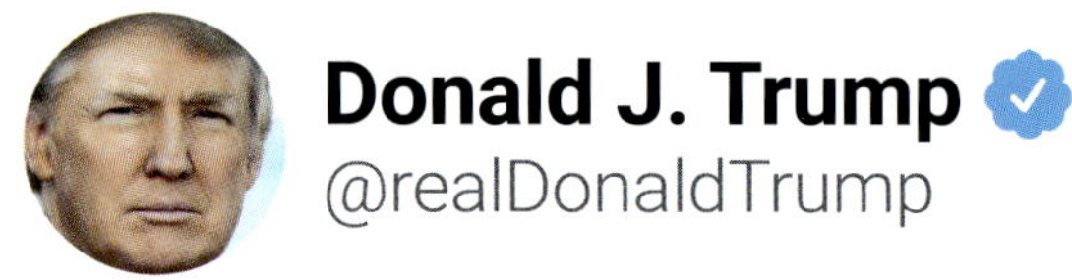

Donald J. Trump
@realDonaldTrump

I WON THIS ELECTION, BY A LOT!

10:36 AM • Nov 7, 2020

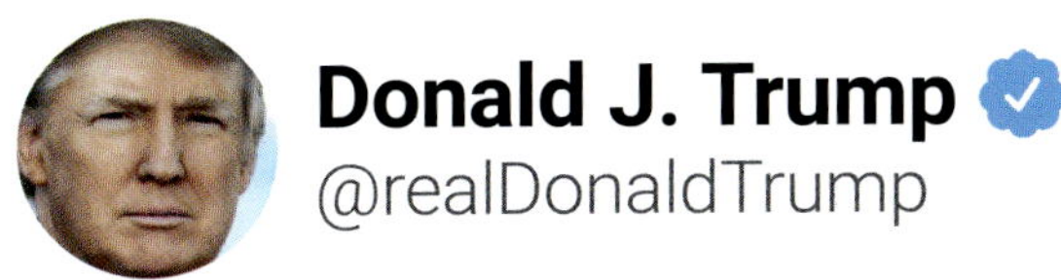

Donald J. Trump ✓
@realDonaldTrump

71,000,000 Legal Votes. The most EVER for a sitting
President!

4:54 PM · Nov 7, 2020

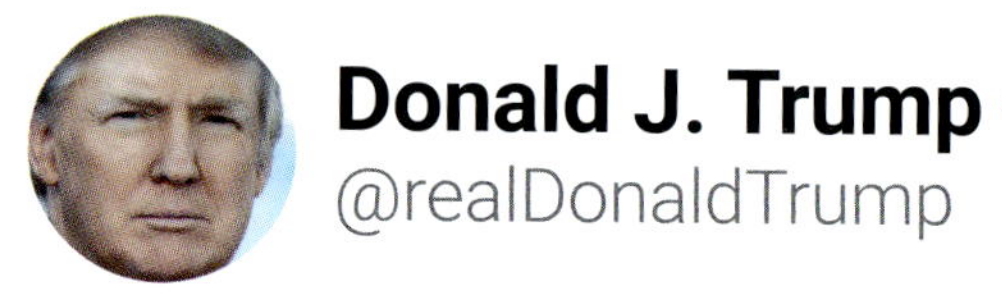
Donald J. Trump
@realDonaldTrump
RIGGED ELECTION. WE WILL WIN!
9:16 AM · Nov 15, 2020

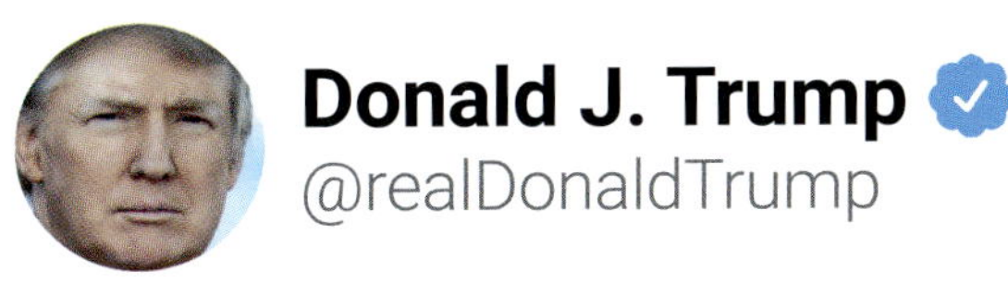

He only won in the eyes of the FAKE NEWS MEDIA. I concede NOTHING! We have a long way to go. This was a RIGGED ELECTION!

9:19 AM · Nov 15, 2020

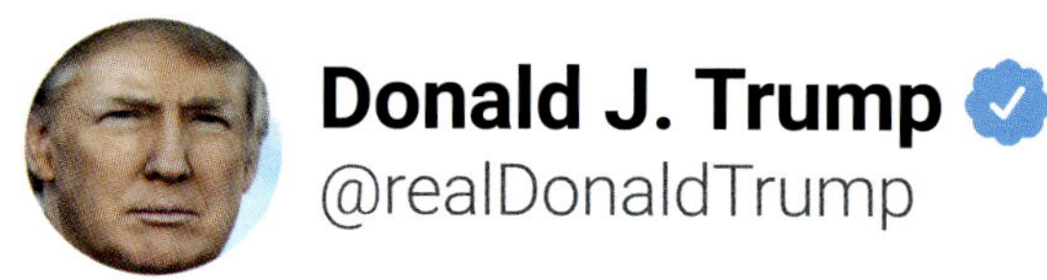

Donald J. Trump
@realDonaldTrump

AMERICA FIRST!!!

4:46 PM · Nov 24, 2020

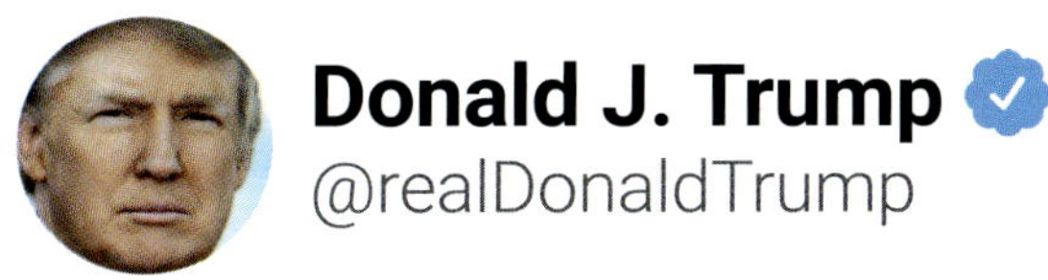

Donald J. Trump
@realDonaldTrump

Just saw the vote tabulations. There is NO WAY Biden got 80,000,000 votes!!! This was a 100% RIGGED ELECTION.

10:44 AM · Nov 26, 2020

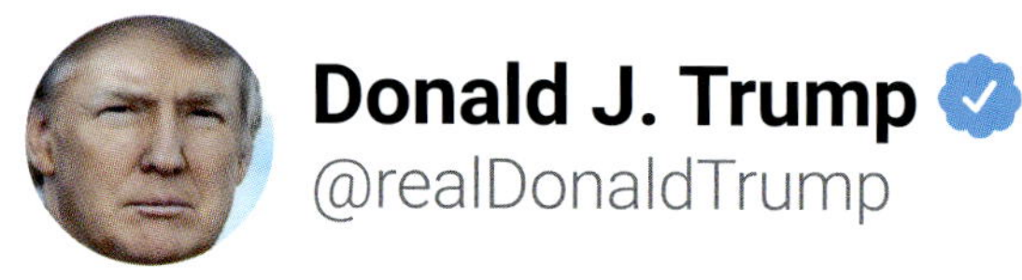

Donald J. Trump @realDonaldTrump

GET TOUGH REPUBLICANS!

8:54 AM · Dec 4, 2020

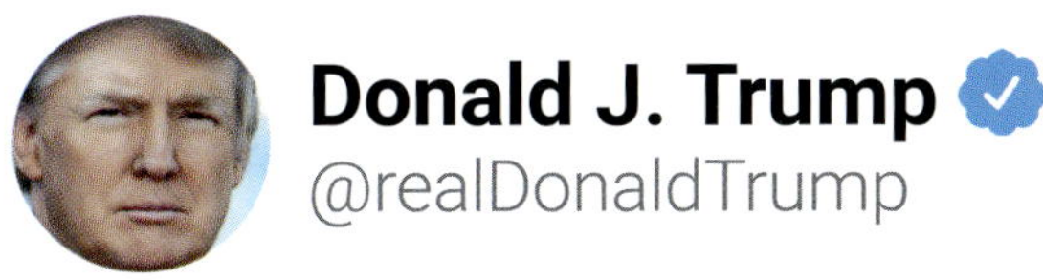

I just want to stop the world from killing itself!

7:26 AM · Dec 11, 2020

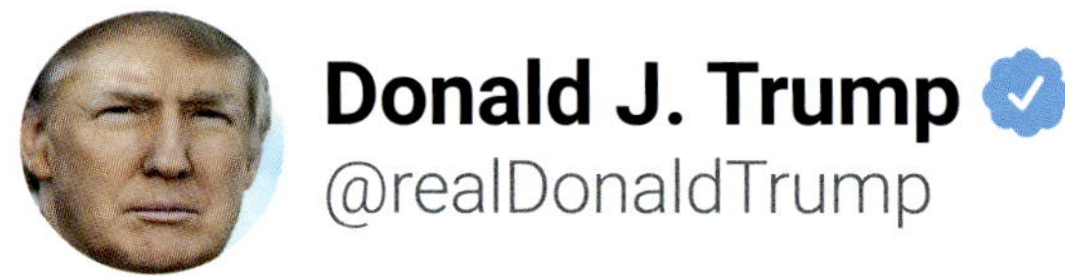

Donald J. Trump
@realDonaldTrump

WE HAVE JUST BEGUN TO FIGHT!!!

8:47 AM · Dec 12, 2020

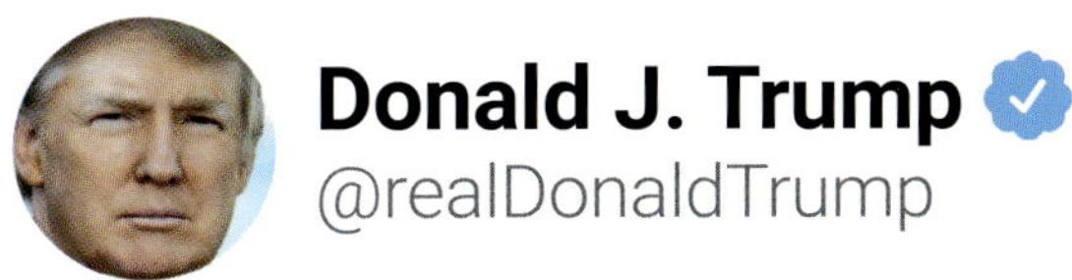

MOST CORRUPT ELECTION IN U.S. HISTORY!

10:36 AM · Dec 13, 2020

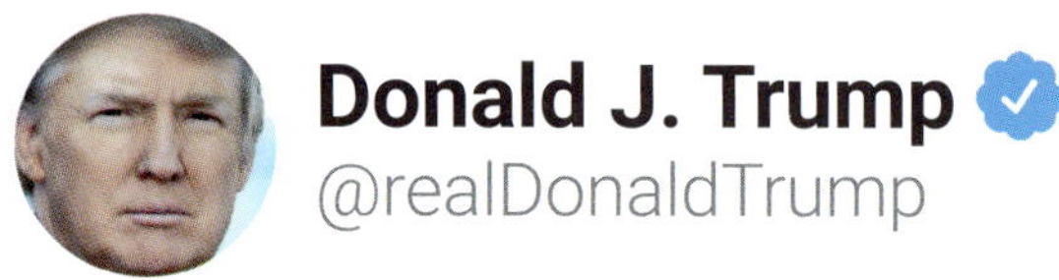

Donald J. Trump ✔
@realDonaldTrump

VOTER FRAUD IS NOT A CONSPIRACY THEORY, IT IS A FACT!!!

3:56 PM · Dec 24, 2020

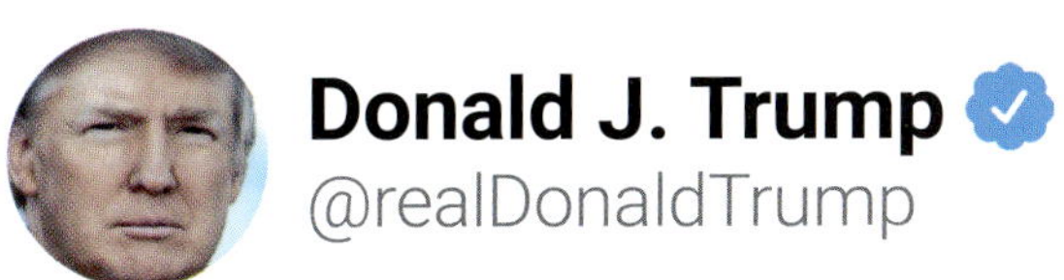

Donald J. Trump ✔
@realDonaldTrump

Twitter is going wild with their flags, trying hard to suppress even the truth. Just shows how dangerous they are, purposely stifling free speech. Very dangerous for our Country. Does Congress know that this is how Communism starts? Cancel Culture at its worst. End Section 230!

5:59 PM · Dec 24, 2020

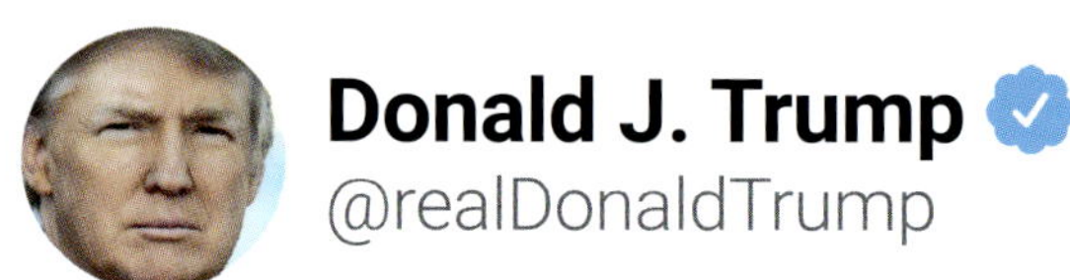

A young military man working in Afghanistan told me that elections in Afghanistan are far more secure and much better run than the USA's 2020 Election. Ours, with its millions and millions of corrupt Mail-In Ballots, was the election of a third world country. Fake President!

9:00 AM • Dec 26, 2020

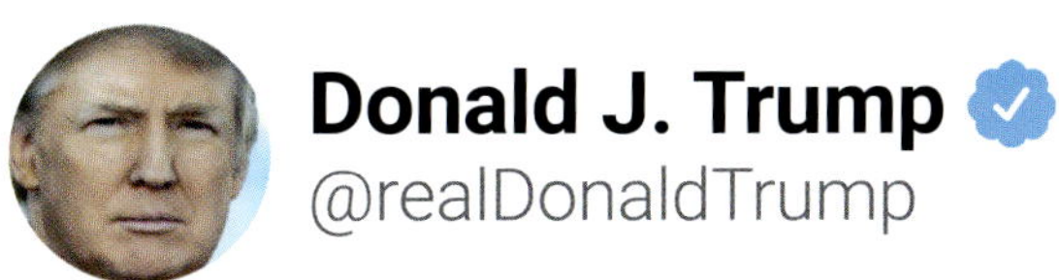

Donald J. Trump ✓
@realDonaldTrump

Twitter is shadow banning like never before. A disgrace that our weak and ineffective political leadership refuses to do anything about Big Tech. They're either afraid or stupid, nobody really knows!

2:05 PM · Dec 30, 2020

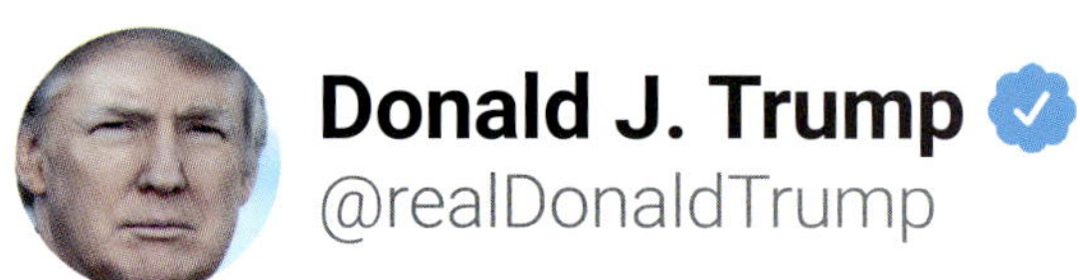

The number of cases and deaths of the China Virus is far exaggerated in the United States because of @CDCgov's ridiculous method of determination compared to other countries, many of whom report, purposely, very inaccurately and low. "When in doubt, call it Covid." Fake News!

8:14 AM · Jan 3, 2021

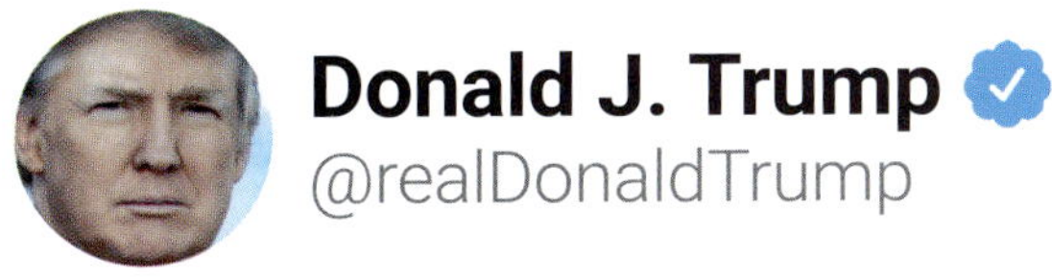

Even Mexico uses Voter I.D.

9:16 AM • Jan 6, 2021

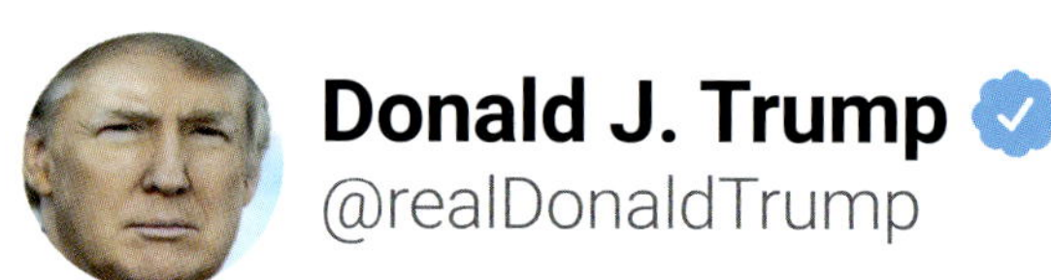

These are the things and events that happen when a sacred landslide election victory is so unceremoniously & viciously stripped away from great patriots who have been badly & unfairly treated for so long. Go home with love & in peace. Remember this day forever!

6:01 PM • Jan 6, 2021

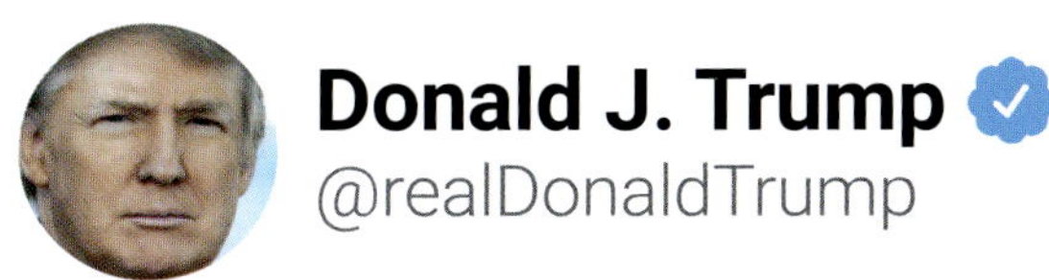

The 75,000,000 great American Patriots who voted for me, AMERICA FIRST, and MAKE AMERICA GREAT AGAIN, will have a GIANT VOICE long into the future. They will not be disrespected or treated unfairly in any way, shape or form!!!

9:46 AM • Jan 8, 2021

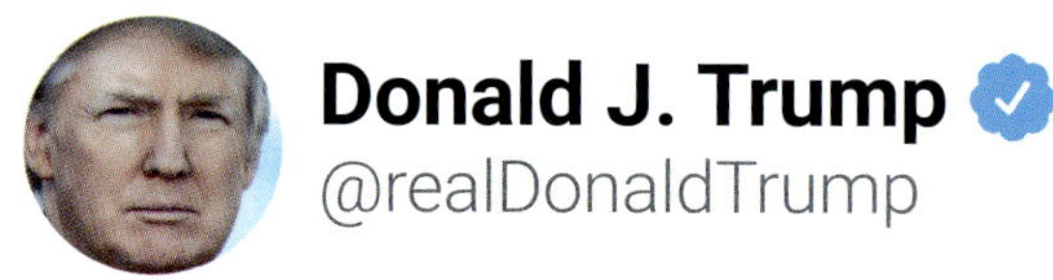

To all of those who have asked, I will not be going to the Inauguration on January 20th.

10:44 AM • Jan 8, 2021

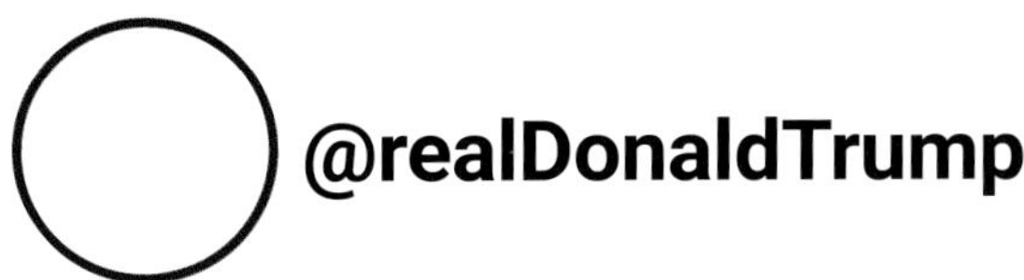 **@realDonaldTrump**

Account suspended

Twitter suspends accounts which violate the Twitter Rules

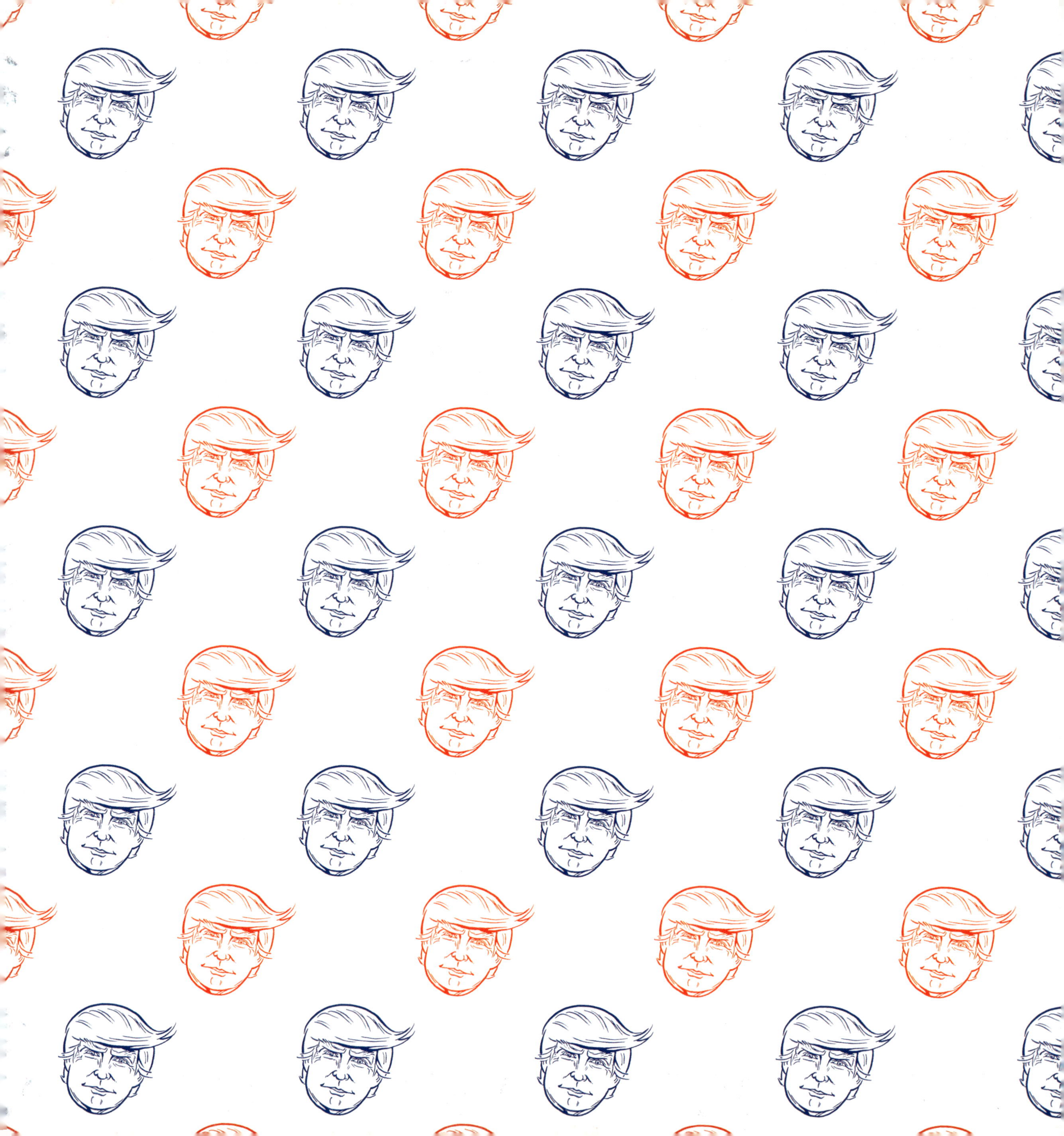